STERLING W. SILL

THE
WEALTH
OF WISDOM

Published by Deseret Book Company, Salt Lake City, Utah, 1977

Contents

1
LEARNING WISDOM FROM OTHERS

2
DEVELOPING OUR PERSONALITIES WITH WISDOM

3

USING WISDOM IN OUR ACTIONS

4

BUILDING WISDOM INTO OUR SOULS

1

LEARNING WISDOM FROM OTHERS

"And as all have not faith,
seek ye diligently and teach one another
words of wisdom; yea, seek ye out of
the best books words of wisdom;
seek learning, even by study
and also by faith."

Our Wisdom Literature

In that period of our world's history between 200 B.C. and A.D. 100, a great deal of religious writing came into being that has been referred to as the wisdom literature of the Hebrews. Some of this is now found in the Apocrypha, which contains a number of books that were not included in the Bible.

The wisdom literature of this and other periods contains philosophies that express, by means of proverbs, sermons, and fables, the results of the reflections of wise men concerning the general questions of life. The writers of the wisdom literature made use of the scriptures, including the writings of the prophets, as well as many others noted for their excellent counsel and good judgment.

Today as in the past, wise men give counsel through their writings. Wisdom literature is not all religious writing. The Master himself spent much of his time speaking of the activities of the sower, the prodigal son, the good Samaritan. He told inspiring parables about the lilies of the field, the good husbandman, the vine-dresser's sons. A poet has said:

He spake of lilies, vines and corn,
The sparrow and the raven,
Things so wonderous and so wise,
Were on men's hearts engraven.

We who live today, in this age of the greatest of all knowledge explosions, have access to untold amounts of wisdom literature applying to our health, our occupations, our minds, and our souls, and we should be more appreciative than anyone else has ever been of important ideas.

1

In some eras and societies, human wisdom and divine wisdom have been regarded as being opposed to each other. This is not necessarily so. In the Apocrypha, wisdom literature generally, and even the scriptures themselves, we find many statements to the effect that wisdom is the one virtue that is indispensable to the human being who would lead a godly life, a life of excellence.

One of the prominent writers of the wisdom literature of the early period was Simeon, the son of Jeshua, who was called Ben-Sira. He was the author of the Sirach, or Ben-Sira's Book of Wisdom. Ben-Sira was a constructor of wise sayings and uplifting philosophies. He belonged to the class of sages who in the days of Jeremiah occupied recognized positions alongside the priests and the prophets. His book of wisdom contains moral axioms and wise counsels regarding almost every conceivable situation in life. Like many other constructive thinkers, Ben-Sira expanded some of these proverbs into stimulating essays. To Ben-Sira, even the most secular forms of wisdom partake of something that is fundamentally religious, and he may have been anticipating the Lord's statement that to Him "all things are spiritual," for certainly wisdom is an offshoot of that wisdom which emanates from God. Wise maxims and counsels may be applied to people in every condition of life. Most of them deal with the ordinary, everyday relationships between persons, whether in regard to the rich or the poor, the oppressed, those who mourn, rules of courtesy and politeness, respect for one's betters, kindness, and other similar topics.

Knowledge of human nature requires one's attention in every step of our life's journey. It was clearly Ben-Sira's objective in writing his book to present to the people of his day an authoritative work of reference to which recourse could be had for guidance and instruction in every circumstance of life.

2

The people of his period were faithful to the law, the ordinances of which were binding because they were the revealed will of God. As Solomon, another writer of wisdom literature, pointed out, "The fear of the Lord is the beginning of wisdom." (Proverbs 9:10.) By the fear of the Lord is meant a personal law of God, obedience to the divine commandments, and observance of the law. Truth is the finest expression of any wisdom literature.

Just as the wisdom literature and consciousness of it influenced the Hebrews, so we today ought to think and write and aspire to make our own wisdom literature and become conscious with it and identify with it.

For each of our individual activities, we should ask ourselves, Is it right? Is it wise? Is it helpful? Is it profitable? Our small troubles may be the result of our imprudence; more serious troubles may result from wrong doing. Therefore, to be wise we should avoid imprudence as well as abstain from evil. Our wisdom literature may be represented by the philosophies of ancient times, but it should motivate us to a greater, fuller recognition of wise ideas and activities for our own life and time. Let us each strive to make ourselves worthy of the designation of wise men. Let us strive always to follow the counsel of the Lord, who in our day declared: ". . . seek ye diligently and teach one another words of wisdom; yea, seek ye out of the best books words of wisdom; seek learning, even by study and also by faith." (D&C 88:118.)

3

The World's
First Book of Wisdom

The Bible is probably the world's most useful and worthwhile resource. It accounts for many of the differences found in human lives. When peoples have lived without the word of the Lord, they have usually soon dwindled in unbelief and marched along that road that has led them to degradation and the fall of their civilization.

In attempting to measure the benefits of following the precepts of the Bible, compare the Christian attitudes of the American founding fathers, who built a nation on a foundation of belief in God, with the objectives of such godless men as Hitler, Stalin, and some of our present-day dictators. Without divine guidance, men and women are likely to lose the spirit of righteousness as well as their human dignity, liberty, and free agency. We see a reflection of biblical values in Abraham Lincoln, who translated its benefits into his own life and made them serve his country's welfare. As he was freeing the slaves he said, "As I would not be a slave, so I would not be a master." Many other great men have been able to utilize the godly virtues mentioned in the holy scriptures and make them negotiable in their own lives and the lives of others.

Surveys show that a large percentage of the people who live in the United States at least claim to believe in the Bible. Many accept it as the word of God. The actual number is much smaller of those who effectively study it and do what it says, so that they get its fullest benefit. We can only imagine what our society would actually be like if every citizen enthusiastically and wholeheartedly believed in God.

It is comparatively easy to believe in the Bible as a distant object of adoration. When it sits unopened on the

4

shelf, the effects of its doctrines are often too indefinite to cause a conflict in our minds. And when there is no pressure to put its commandments into actual operation, we are inclined to think it is a wonderful book. But when the Bible is opened, with its doctrines exposed and its philosophies inviting practice, then we sometimes lose some of our enthusiasm. Therefore, even though the Bible remains our greatest possession, we lose much of its value when we do not fully accept its theology and fully practice its teachings. When we follow the process of partial enthusiasm and fractional obedience, we are wasting some of our greatest resources.

The Bible is not only the world's first book of religion; it is also the world's first book of philosophy. It is the world's first book of history. It is the world's first book of culture. It is the world's first book of literature. Many great writers repeatedly refer to the Bible. Jesus himself quoted from the Old Testament 89 times. The works of Shakespeare contain 550 quotations and allusions to the Bible. The writings of Emerson are filled with many ideas and philosophies from the Bible. The poetry of Tennyson contains 330 Bible references. The Bible is one of the most significant miracles of all ages.

Even though the Bible was written when the camel was the chief means of transportation, in many respects this book is even more up-to-date today than it would have been if it had been written yesterday, for many of the events discussed in it are still awaiting fulfillment. The Bible contains many inspired teachings about the relationship existing between God and ourselves, and many of its instructions were written specifically for our own day and beyond.

Some Bible prophecies are presently being fulfilled. In other chapters we may look ahead to such over-whelming events as the cleansing of this earth by fire in preparation for the glorious coming of Christ with his holy angels to reign upon the earth during its promised millennium of a thousand years of peace. The Bible also tells of such personal events as our own resurrection and the conditions surrounding our eternal future destiny.

The Bible is the world's first book of success. The very best way to be a good lawyer or a good teacher or a good businessman is to be a good man, and the Bible is filled with many teachings about both goodness and greatness. All we need to do is just get them out of the Bible and into ourselves.

The Bible is the world's first book of wisdom. When we read it with the idea of getting its wisdom, it becomes a different kind of book than if we read it for its poetry or its history or even its theology. Because we usually find those things that we earnestly look for, one who strictly lives by the Ten Commandments, the Sermon on the Mount, and the other sacred writings cannot help but be a wise man. Wisdom and righteousness are synonymous, as are wickedness and unrighteous behavior.

The wisdom of the Bible has scarcely been touched. / It has thousands of inspiring stories, commandments, / and philosophies capable of upgrading the lives and / glorifying the spirit and activities of everyone who will / make an effort to get on intimate terms with it.

Many great lessons may be learned from reading the Bible. For example, when Moses was starting across the desert with his vast company of people, he needed someone who knew the desert to serve as their guide. There was a man living on the edge of the desert by the name of Hobab, whose services Moses desired to obtain. Moses said to him, ". . . come with us, and we will do thee good." Hobab replied, "I will not go." However, because Moses desperately needed Hobab, he tried again. This time he altered his approach and said, ". . . thou mayest be to us instead of eyes." (Numbers 10:29-31.) In this he used an entirely different appeal. When Moses had tried to induce Hobab saying, "We will do thee good," Hobab was not impressed.

Most people are not generally attracted by do-good programs. Yet we are still making this kind of appeal in many places today, frequently without success. For example, we say to a prospective church member, "You come to church and we will do thee good." In other words, we strongly infer that we are nice people and it would do you good to be associated with us. That may be entirely true, but this appeal usually doesn't have very much power. However, when Moses told Hobab that he would be as eyes to them in the wilderness, he was saying, "Hobab, come and be our leader. You know the desert better than we do, and we will probably get lost without you to show us the way." Translated into our language, this says, "You come and teach this class in religion or lead this cultural or recreational activity. You have an ability that we don't have, and we need you to be our eyes in the wilderness." This appeal to serve was too strong for Hobab to resist, and he was soon on his way guiding the children of Israel toward their promised land. Like Hobab, most people respond more readily to an invitation to serve than one to be served.

The Bible teaches many success principles. For example, it tells us:

1. Do unto others as you would have others do unto you.
2. All things work together for the good of them that love God.
3. Be of good cheer.
4. All things are possible to him that believeth.
5. Be not afraid.
6. Follow the Savior.
7. Love your enemies.
8. Blessed is he who is not offended.
9. Seek first the kingdom of God and his righteousness.
10. He that loseth his life for Jesus' sake shall find it.
11. Man does not live by bread alone.

The Bible is the word of the Lord. It contains the greatest program ever written on the greatest of all subjects—eternal progression. We have the promise that if we do certain things we will be resurrected, glorified, and become even as God is. Certainly one of our greatest opportunities is to study this tremendous *wonder* volume and make it a part of our lives.

The Great Teacher

Some 2700 years ago, as the prophet Isaiah looked forward to the coming of Christ, he foretold some of the important things about the Savior, including some of the titles by which he would be known. He said, "For unto us a child is born, unto us a son is given: and the government shall be upon his shoulder: and his name shall be called Wonderful, Counsellor, The mighty God, The everlasting Father, The Prince of Peace. Of the increase of his government and peace there shall be no end. . . ." (Isaiah 9:6-7.) In his antemortal life the Christ was ordained to be the Savior of the world and the Redeemer of men. He has been called the Master and the Great Physician. One of the most magnificent of his titles is that of the Great Teacher.

In a revelation given to Moses, God the Father said of the antemortal Christ, then known as Jehovah, "And worlds without number have I created; . . . and by the Son I created them, which is my Only Begotten." (Moses 1:33.) Even before Bethlehem, Christ was a Creator of worlds. He was the second member of the Godhead, which served as the presidency of heaven. He ruled with God the Father long before this earth itself was formed. He was appointed by the Father to have direct charge of the affairs of our earth. He was the God of Abraham, Isaac, and Jacob. Some fifteen centuries B.C. he came down onto the top of Mt. Sinai in a cloud of fire with such power that the mountain shook and the people trembled. Among other things, to the accompaniment of the thunders and lightnings of that holy mountain, he said, "Thou shalt have no other gods before me." (Exodus 20:3.) Just think of the tremendous progress we would make if we always followed that one direction given by this greatest intelligence of heaven next to the Father himself. This earth would then soon become God's paradise.

In the meridian of time Jehovah, the first begotten Son of God in the spirit, took upon himself mortality and became known to us upon this earth as Jesus Christ.

One of Jesus' primary responsibilities was that of teaching. As he finished his life's work upon this earth and prepared to ascend to his Father from Mount Olivet, he passed this teaching commission on to those he had prepared for this assignment. He said to those leaders who stood at his feet: "Go ye therefore, and teach all nations, baptizing them in the name of the Father, and of the Son, and of the Holy Ghost: . . . and lo, I am with you alway, even to the end of the world." (Matthew 28: 19-20.) He said: "He that believeth and is baptized shall be saved; but he that believeth not shall be damned." (Mark 16:16.) This commission has now been passed on to us.

Dr. Henry C. Link once said, "Nothing puts so much order into human life as to live by a set of sound principles." The soundest principles ever known in the universe are the principles of the gospel of Jesus Christ. Each one has an important purpose, and we receive miraculous power when we make them a part of us.

When the Prophet Joseph Smith was asked how he taught a divergent group of people, members of The Church of Jesus Christ of Latter-day Saints, he said, "I teach them correct principles, and they govern themselves."

Teaching correct principles to his children is probably the most important function of God himself. But, like so many others, this is a function that he shares with us. He has appointed teachers among his children to carry on this process of imparting knowledge and fostering development.

What a great good fortune it is to have wonderful parents who are good teachers of righteousness and truth. In addition to having parents who set good examples, we are also blessed if we have good teachers in our youth, teachers who enlarge our vision and stimulate our minds.

Of course, not all great teachers are employed in classrooms. Some of the greatest lessons of my life I learned from a bishop, from a Scoutmaster, and from my employer out on the farm. On my own, I have taken some courses from Shakespeare, Emerson, Elbert Hubbard, Harry Emerson Fosdick, the apostle Paul, the prophet Job, the prophet Moses, and a humble fisherman by the name of Simon Peter. What a thrill it is just to think that at our own pleasure we can select the greatest minds that have ever lived upon the earth and learn their greatest lessons!

God has provided us with many other kinds of teachers. One of the most powerful of these is that of our own experience. We could give ourselves a substantial advantage in life by keeping track of uplifting experiences in our lives with some pointed notes about what we have learned from each of them. It is one of the good fortunes of our lives that we can learn to do by doing. We can also learn from having anticipations and motivating expectations. Actually we are our own greatest teachers.

Another important teacher is industry. Industry is a parent virtue, and when we really learn how to work, then any accomplishment is placed within our reach. Industry is one variety of genius. It has been said that "genius is the power to make continuous effort," and "the secret of success is constancy of purpose." Obedience is a great teacher. Faith is a great teacher. Habit is a great teacher. Example is a great teacher. As the poet has said:

Example sheds a genial ray of light
Which men are apt to borrow,
So first improve yourselves today
And then improve your friends tomorrow.

Inspiring associates with whom we work are great teachers. More or less unconsciously, even to ourselves, we absorb from them that which is inspirational, uplifting, helpful, and profitable to us.

All of the great virtues are also parent virtues, and they beget the most wonderful offspring in their own image. However, we ourselves are the only ones who can actually bring about our own success. We are the only ones who can properly prepare the mental soil where real learning takes place most effectively. No one can do our studying for us. No one can do our thinking for us.

No one except ourselves can shape our attitudes or form our determinations. A good teacher should know much about the student, but a good teacher should also know much about himself. This is particularly true when we are going to function in both roles at the same time.

There are certain procedures that can make learning more pleasant and easy, and if we get ourselves in the right mood and generate the right kind of ambition we can succeed. We should always serve God, and as our own teacher and the one who controls our own destiny, we ourselves should intervene endlessly and vigorously in our own behalf to bring ourselves to that great destination where we will all someday want to be.

The Wisdom of Jesus

The greatest being who ever lived upon our earth was born nearly two thousand years ago in Bethlehem of Judea and was known as Jesus of Nazareth. He was the first begotten and most capable son of God in the spirit, and he was appointed by the Father and ratified by the premortal council of heaven to be the Savior of the world and the Redeemer of men.

He was associated with the Father as the Creator of our world. It was under his direction that Lucifer was banished from heaven because of his rebellion against God. During his short life, and his shorter ministry, he was known as the Great Teacher, the Great Physician. He was the Light of the world and the Master of men.

During his premortal state, he had been associated in the Godhead with his Father and the Holy Spirit. He has all knowledge and all power; he is all good, and one of the thoughts that gives me one of my greatest comforts is to think of him in his state of being all-wise. Out of his wisdom, under the direction of the Father, he created this earth. He organized the principles of life and happiness that we know as the principles of the gospel of Jesus Christ. He has also made us the beneficiaries of his abilities and virtues, and has indicated that someday even we may become like him if we fully follow his direction.

We sing a song in which we say, "Cast thy burdens on the Lord." The Lord himself said it this way: "Take my yoke upon you, and learn of me; . . . For my yoke is easy, and my burden is light." (Matthew 11:29-30.) How thrilling it is to know we may be entitled to be inspired by him and be uplifted by his example and make ourselves the beneficiaries of his all-knowing wisdom. We have also been promised that if we are worthy, we will have the inspiration of the Holy Spirit to guide us in all our activities.

The scripture says, ". . . there is a spirit in man: and the inspiration of the Almighty giveth them understanding." (Job 32:8.) How necessary it is that we learn to keep our lives and minds open always to the promptings of the Spirit!

We might go back and review, as we know it, the earthly ministry of the Savior of the world. Certainly our capacity is increased as we learn to appreciate the many blessings available from him. Of his early life in Nazareth, we know very little. However, the scriptures make some significant statements about him, including the following: "And the child grew, and waxed strong in spirit, filled with wisdom: and the grace of God was upon him." (Luke 2:40.) The scriptures put great emphasis on wisdom as one of the leading characteristics of the Master of all mankind. Luke makes another statement about it when he says: "And Jesus increased in wisdom and stature, and in favour with God and man." (Luke 2:52.) That is the kind of development that all of us should be aware of and working toward. It indicates increase in mental development, physical development, and spiritual development. These references both mention Jesus' wisdom, and about the only other thing that the New Testament tells us about the early life of Jesus is his experience of teaching the wise men in the temple when he was twelve years of age.

What could be more important than these all-wise, all-knowing, all-good characteristics of him who is our Creator and Redeemer and the one working to bring about our eternal exaltation. In every way, Jesus taught us to always use good judgment and to learn to reason logically and think effectively. We learn wisdom by practice and by being obedient to wise instruction. He taught us to study. He said, ". . . seek ye out of the best books words of wisdom; seek learning, even by study and also by faith." (D&C 88:118.) ← ✗ ✗ ✗

Jesus gave the greatest success formula of all ages in just two words when he said, "Follow me." How important it is for us to follow him in his faith, in his industry, in his righteousness, in his thoughtfulness.

He was teaching us preparation when he told the parable of the wise and foolish virgins. (Matthew 25:2.) He was doing the same thing when he taught about the faithful and wise steward. (Luke 12:42.) Usually we don't fall down in life because of our sins. Our biggest problems come because we are unwise. The more foolish things we do, the more unwise we become. The more wise things we do, the wiser we become. Wisdom feeds upon itself, and so do sin and foolishness and bad judgment. If we sin today, the habit gets a little deeper and tomorrow's sins come easier. The Ten Commandments are wise statements, and we should make no exceptions in being obedient to their precepts. When we make exceptions, we tear the good habits down and build the bad habits up.

We should also keep all of the other directions of the Lord. Think of the wisdom of the parables, the inspiration of the Beatitudes (beautiful attitudes), the great principles of salvation, eternal progresson, literal bodily resurrection, the blessings of the celestial kingdom. The very best way to be a wise man in heaven is to be a wise man here on earth. That is what Jesus had in mind when he said we should live by every word that proceedeth forth from the mouth of God.

He has said, "Whatever principle of intelligence we attain unto in this life, it will rise with us in the resurrection. And if a person gains more knowledge and intelligence in this life through his diligence and obedience than another, he will have so much the advantage in the world to come." (D&C 130:18-19.) He will also have many advantages in this world.

To develop wisdom is the way to wealth. It is the way to health. It is the way to happiness and success. It is the way to knowledge and power and fulfillment. Let us start working at it more diligently immediately, since any procrastination may lead to our doom. Solomon said, "With all thy getting, get understanding." And someone who may have been wise like Solomon said, "With all thy getting, get going."

The Wisdom of Job

One of my favorites of the Old Testament personalities is the prophet Job. Even among the giant luminaries that light up the pages of holy scripture, Job stands out like a bright beacon.

We are introduced to him in the first chapter of the Old Testament book that bears his name, where the record says, "There was a man in the land of Uz, whose name was Job: and that man was perfect and upright, and one that feared God, and eschewed evil." (Job 1:1.) He was a very wise man, a great prophet, and an outstanding family man. Because of his thoughtful planning and vigorous industry, he was also a very wealthy property owner.

Job loved God and all righteousness. He possessed the most admirable qualities of character. In him we see love, righteousness, faith, understanding, patience, and sympathy with his fellowmen.

A predominating theme of his book centers in that

15

eternal question concerning the purpose of human suffering, either merited or not merited. Suffering frequently is purifying to our souls if we have the right attitude about it. The scripture says even of Jesus, ". . . yet learned he obedience by the things which he suffered." (Hebrews 5:8.) Probably next only to the Master himself we think of Job as heading the list so far as human suffering and the excellence of his attitude about it are concerned.

One of the most thrilling ideas in the holy scriptures so far as I am concerned is spoken by Job when, in the midst of his troubles and afflictions, he lets us feel the strength and power of his godly attitude as he says, "All the while my breath is in me, and the spirit of God is in my nostrils; My lips shall not speak wickedness, nor my tongue utter deceit. . . . till I die I will not remove mine integrity from me. My righteousness I hold fast, and will not let it go: my heart shall not reproach me so long as I live." (Job 27:3-6.)

Under the pressure of a little adversity or trouble many people adopt the foolish attitudes of anger and bitterness and blame everybody else for their problems. Job's friends tried unsuccessfully to get him to adopt this negative, destructive attitude. Even his wife said to him, ". . . curse God and die" (Job 2:9), but Job pointed out that he had received many good things from the hand of God and that he ought to be able to stand up like a man under a little adversity.

Job had thrilling faith in God. He said to God, "I know that thou canst do every thing. . . ." (Job 42:2.) And whether he understood the purpose of his own suffering or not, he would not abandon his integrity or his faith, for he said of God, "Though he slay me, yet will I trust in him. . . ." (Job 13:15.)

God also paid Job one of the greatest compliments when he asked Satan, "Hast thou considered my servant Job, that there is none like him in the earth, a perfect and an upright man, one that feareth God, and escheweth evil?" (Job 1:8.) Satan tried to argue that Job's piety depended upon his prosperity, and that if Job should find himself in difficulties, he would abandon his allegiance to God.

There are many people who follow their religion as a sharp, unethical businessman would pursue his business opportunities. He would make the best deals he could but would turn away and do other things if they did not seem to secure for him an advantage.

And so God permitted Satan to take from Job everything that he had except his life. But Job stood up to the situation with great strength and determination. He said, "Naked came I out of my mother's womb, and naked shall I return thither: the Lord gave, and the Lord hath taken away; blessed be the name of the Lord." (Job 1:21.)

Over the ages, Job has been characterized chiefly by his patience, but his character was also rich in integrity and wisdom. The Lord himself asked Job some searching questions. He said, "Where wast thou when I laid the foundations of the earth? declare, if thou hast understanding. Who hath laid the measures thereof, if thou knowest? or who hath stretched the line upon it? Whereupon are the foundations thereof fastened? or who laid the corner stone thereof; When the morning stars sang together, and all the sons of God shouted for joy?" (Job 38:4-7.)

Jesus said, "And this is life eternal, that they might know thee the only true God, and Jesus Christ, whom thou hast sent." (John 17:3.) We should also know about the laws of God and his program for our own lives. The Lord wanted Job to know about his antemortal existence. That is just as important for us, for we also were present in that council of God when the foundations of this earth were being laid; and when we knew that we were going to have the privilege of coming to the earth and living

17

upon it and having the privilege of taking advantage of the opportunities of our second estate, no wonder "the morning stars sang together and all the sons of God shouted for joy"!

The book of Job poses some other questions. For example, "Canst [a man] by searching find out God?" (Job 11:7.) Human wisdom is a weak and fragile thing compared to the wisdom of the Divine, but Job points out that there is a spirit in man, and the inspiration of the Almighty giveth it understanding. If we keep God's commandments, he will reveal himself and his programs to us. He will help us to discover the secrets of wisdom.

Job was confronted with another question: "If a man die, shall he live again?" (Job 14:14.) Many people in the world do not know the answer to this famous question, and yet almost no other could be as important. There are some who would give a negative answer. There are some who believe in an eternal life on a basis so weak and indefinite that it has little power to upgrade their lives. As there is wisdom in knowing about our premortal states, so there is wisdom in knowing about our eternal postmortal estate. God himself said, "For as in Adam all die, even so in Christ shall all be made alive." (1 Corinthians 15:22.) God has ordained the literal bodily resurrection and the eternity of the family relationship. How much wiser we are in handling our problems when we know and understand the answers to these questions!

Now feel the enthusiasm of the faith of Job, who lived many generations before the resurrection was initiated upon this earth. He said, "Oh that my words were now written! oh that they were printed in a book! That they were graven with an iron pen and lead in the rock for ever! For I know that my redeemer liveth, and that he shall stand at the latter day upon the earth: And though my skin worms destroy this body, yet in my flesh shall I see God: Whom I shall see for myself, and mine eyes shall behold, and not another; though my reins be consumed within me." (Job 19:23-27.)

In order to increase the quality of wisdom within himself, Job spent a great deal of time meditating about the values of life. He asked himself some very important questions and insisted upon training himself to give the right answers. This procedure and the questions themselves might serve us as advantageously as they did him, if we would go about it in the same way. Job said, "But where shall wisdom be found? and where is the place of understanding?" (Job 28:12.) He might also have said, "How can we find and develop both of these important qualities?" What a wonderful asset we ourselves could have if we would get a proper testimony about these important subjects for ourselves instead of the weak attitude we might acquire by allowing the answers to skate too lightly across the surface of our minds!

Job asked another important question when he said, "Can a man be profitable unto God, as he that is wise may be profitable unto himself? Is it any pleasure to the Almighty, that thou art righteous? or is it a gain to him, that thou makest thy ways perfect?" (Job 22:2-3.) If a man does the right thing he can be very profitable unto himself as well as to God.

Job points out that "man knoweth not the price" of wisdom. He said, "It cannot be gotten for gold, neither shall silver be weighed for the price thereof. It cannot be valued with the gold of Ophir." He said, ". . . the price of wisdom is above rubies." (Job 28:13, 16, 18.)

We can easily understand this idea because, while wisdom can produce wealth, wealth cannot produce wisdom. Therefore wisdom is greater than wealth. Wisdom can also produce love and righteousness. What a great bargain it would be if we could buy unerring wisdom with money, with labor, with education, or even with our own blood, sweat, toil, and tears. To help us get the right answer, we ought to meditate more upon

19

Job's question and try to discover the answers to this important proclamation: "Whence then cometh wisdom? and where is the place of understanding?" (Job 28:20.) If we could personally get some good answers to those questions, we would be well on our way to the most outstanding personal joy.

As a proof of his own wisdom, Job said, ". . . the fear of the Lord, that is wisdom; and to depart from evil is understanding." (Job 28:28.) He might also have said, "Obedience to God is wisdom," "Living the principles of the gospel is wisdom," "Righteous industry is wisdom."

More than just about anything else, God our Eternal Heavenly Father wants each one of us to build solid qualities in our characters. He wants us to be fully informed, fully righteous, fully thoughtful. He wants us always to use good judgment, with love in our hearts for good things.

After Job had passed all his tests, he was given twice as much in material things as he had had before. He was also much wiser. The record says, "So the Lord blessed the latter end of Job more than his beginnings." (Job 42:12.) And God will similarly bless us if we are diligent in developing the excellence of our wisdom.

The Wisdom of Solomon

One of the most famous men who has ever lived upon the earth was Solomon, the son of David, who was born around 1000 B.C. David, his famous father, had succeeded in consolidating the nation of Israel by driving out the hostile tribes in a long series of wars and had established his capital at Jerusalem. As David neared the end of his life, he said to Solomon:

20

"I go the way of all the earth: be thou strong therefore, and shew thyself a man;

"And keep the charge of the Lord thy God, to walk in his way, to keep his statutes, and his commandments, and his judgments, and his testimonies, as it is written in the law of Moses, that thou mayest prosper in all that thou doest, and withersoever thou turnest thyself;

"That the Lord may continue his word which he spake concerning me, saying, if thy children take heed to their way, to walk before me in truth with all their heart and with all their soul, there shall not fail thee (said he) a man on the throne of Israel." (1 Kings 2:2-4.)

Then the record adds, "So David slept with his fathers, and was buried in the city of David." (1 Kings 2:10.) "Then sat Solomon upon the throne of David his father. . . ." (1 Kings 2:12.)

Solomon ascended the throne when he was just a teenager, "and his kingdom was established greatly." (1 Kings 2:12.)

"And Solomon loved the Lord, walking in the statutes of David his Father. . . .

"And the king went to Gibeon to sacrifice there; for that was the great high place: a thousand burnt offerings did Solomon offer upon that altar.

"In Gibeon the Lord appeared to Solomon in a dream by night: and God said, Ask what I shall give thee.

"And Solomon said, Thou hast shewed unto thy servant David my father great mercy, according as he walked before thee in truth, and in righteousness, and in uprightness of heart with thee; and thou hast kept for him this great kindness, that thou hast given him a son to sit on his throne, as it is this day.

"And now, O Lord my God, thou hast made thy servant king instead of David my father: and I am but a little child: I know not how to go out or come in.

"And thy servant is in the midst of thy people which

21

thou hast chosen, a great people that cannot be numbered nor counted for multitude.

"Give therefore thy servant an understanding heart to judge thy people, that I may discern between good and bad: for who is able to judge this thy so great a people?

"And the speech pleased the Lord, that Solomon had asked this thing.

"And God said unto him, Because thou hast asked this thing, and hast not asked for thyself long life; neither hast asked riches for thyself, nor hast asked the life of thine enemies; but hast asked for thyself understanding to discern judgment;

"Behold, I have done according to thy words: lo, I have given thee a wise and an understanding heart; so that there was none like thee before thee, neither after thee shall any arise like unto thee.

"And I have also given thee that which thou hast not asked, both riches, and honor: so that there shall not be any among the kings like unto thee all thy days.

"And if thou wilt walk in my ways, to keep my statutes and my commandments, as thy father David did walk, then I will lengthen thy days." (1 Kings 3:3-14.)

"And the Lord magnified Solomon exceedingly in the sight of all Israel, and bestowed upon him such royal majesty as had not been on any king before him in Israel." (1 Chronicles 29:25.)

"And God gave Solomon wisdom and understanding exceeding much, and largeness of heart, even as the sand that is on the sea shore.

"And Solomon's wisdom excelled the wisdom of all the children of the east country, and all the wisdom of Egypt.

"For he was wiser than all men. . . .

"And he spake three thousand proverbs: and his songs were a thousand and five.

"And he spake of trees, from the cedar tree that is in

22

Lebanon even unto the hyssop that springeth out of the wall: he spake also of beasts, and of fowl, and of creeping things, and of fishes.

"And there came of all people to hear the wisdom of Solomon, from all kings of the earth, which had heard of his wisdom." (1 Kings 4:29-34.)

God also gave Solomon riches and honor, which are the natural result of an understanding heart.

We might, with great profit, study some of the statements made by this favored king, statements that will, if we desire, help us develop some of the by-products of wisdom, such as prestige, power, wealth, and influence. He said:

"Fools despise wisdom and instruction." (Proverbs 1:7.)

"Incline thine ear to wisdom." (Proverbs 2:2.)

"How much better is it to get wisdom than gold!" (Proverbs 16:16.)

Most of the gifts of God do not come to us freely. Most of them require great effort and thoughtfulness on our part. Solomon said:

"I gave my heart to know wisdom." (Ecclesiastes 1:17.)

"Man's wisdom maketh his face to shine." (Ecclesiastes 8:1.)

"The price of wisdom is above rubies." (Proverbs 8:11.)

"Wisdom is better than weapons of war." (Ecclesiastes 9:18.)

"Wisdom is better than strength." (Ecclesiastes 9:16.)

"The fear of the Lord is the beginning of wisdom." (Psalm 111:10, Proverbs 9:10.)

Solomon pointed out one of the chief characteristics of foolishness when he said, "The fool hath said in his heart, There is no God." (Psalm 14:1.) It is very foolish to disbelieve in God, but it is also very foolish to fail to follow his direction. All crime and sin is foolishness.

One of the interesting aspects about the wisdom of Solomon himself is that it turned sour and did not always continue with him. Wisdom can be destroyed by sin and poor judgment, and as Solomon became older, he lost the spirit he had had in his youth. Instead of always acting in harmony with the wisdom with which his life had begun, he did many evil things and died an idolator, very much out of favor with God. As a consequence of this, he, more than anyone else, was responsible for destroying the work of the Lord in ancient Israel, and the kingdom was later divided and both its northern and southern sections were taken into foreign captivity.

The scriptures give us a rather sad obituary for the wisdom by which Solomon had previously been distinguished when it says: "But king Solomon loved many strange women. . . . Of the nations concerning which the Lord said unto the children of Israel, Ye shall not go in to them, neither shall they come in unto you: for surely they will turn away your hearts after their gods. . . .

"For it came to pass, when Solomon was old, that his wives turned away his heart after other gods: and his heart was not perfect with the Lord his God, as was the heart of David his father.

"And Solomon did evil in the sight of the Lord. . . .

"And the Lord was angry with Solomon, because his heart was turned from the Lord God of Israel, which had appeared unto him twice,

"And had commanded him concerning this thing, that he should not go after other gods: but he kept not that which the Lord commanded." (1 Kings 11:1-2, 4, 6, 9-10.)

Solomon's wisdom lacked that qualifying phrase wherein Jesus said, ". . . he that endureth to the end shall be saved." (Matthew 10:22.) Some of the things that led Solomon to this point are indicated by his own statements that, at the very time when he was boasting of his wisdom, he was engaging in unwise practices; he himself said:

"I gave my heart to know wisdom, and to know madness and folly." (Ecclesiastes 1:17.)

"I sought in mine heart to give myself unto wine, . . . and to lay hold on folly. . . .

"Then I saw that wisdom excelleth folly, as far as light excelleth darkness.

"The wise man's eyes are in his head; but the fool walketh in darkness; . . .

"Then said I in my heart, As it happeneth to the fool, so it happeneth even to me. . . .

"Therefore I hated life; because the work that is wrought under the sun is grievous unto me: . . .

"Yea, I hated all my labour which I had taken under the sun: because I should leave [my possessions] unto the man that shall be after me.

"And who knoweth whether he shall be a wise man or a fool? yet shall he rule over all my labour wherein I have laboured, and wherein I have shewed myself wise under the sun. This is also vanity.

"Therefore I went about to cause my heart to despair of all the labour which I took under the sun.

"For there is a man whose labour is in wisdom, and in knowledge, and in equity; yet to a man that hath not laboured therein shall he leave it for his portion. This also is vanity and a great evil." (Ecclesiastes 2:3, 13-15, 17-21.)

"Better is a poor and a wise child than an old and foolish king, who will no more be admonished." (Ecclesiastes 4:13.)

Solomon was speaking from bitter experience when he said: "When thou vowest a vow unto God, defer not to pay it; for he hath no pleasure in fools: pay that which thou hast vowed. Better it is that thou shouldest not vow, than that thou shouldest vow and not pay." (Ecclesiastes 5:4-5.)

In the latter years of Solomon's life he presents a sad picture of wisdom that has gone rancid and turned to folly because he tried to practice during his life both its good and its bad at the same time. Thus he ended up in despair and misery and said of his own life, "Vanity of vanities, . . . All is vanity." (Ecclesiastes 1:2.)

Solomon the wise man seemed to be following the procedure of many people of today who want to try out or experiment with evil. This is a memorable example of what happens when one of the wisest, most powerful men of his day, one whom God loved, was brought down to such a low state that he destroyed the work of his life and died very much out of favor with God.

Socrates

The delights of biography are among the most pleasant in all of human experience. Through books we can enjoy in almost limitless diversity the kind of intimacy with the greatest people of all ages that might have been impossible even to their own next-door neighbors in their own day. We can appropriate their ideas in order to season our own speech and sharpen our own opinions.

One of the most important of our early benefactors answered to the name of Socrates. He lived for seventy-one years in ancient Athens, beginning in the year 470 B.C. His life greatly influenced events that brought about the Golden Age of Greece, and it has enriched all ages since.

Socrates was the son of Sophronicus, the stone-cutter. For some years he followed the trade of his father. Since he was a philosopher at heart, he finally laid down his tools and went out into the marketplace to teach a higher regard for virtue among his contemporaries. Appropriately enough, he was the first man to whom the term "philosopher" was applied. This word comes from Greek words that mean "a lover of wisdom," and certainly no title could have fit him better. To love wisdom is to have the ability to judge soundly and deal sagaciously with facts, especially as they relate to the lives and conduct of people. At every human birth two elements are comingled—a physical body (similar to that possessed by the animals), and a soul (which God shares only with us).

Because Socrates loved to reason, to think, and to understand, he devoted his life to philosophy. It gave him a fine sense of satisfaction to feel maturity and wisdom developing within himself, and he was gratified when he saw such virtues increasing in others. One of the secrets of his successful life was that he treasured knowledge, understanding, fairness, and righteousness.

Many times Socrates mentioned having received promptings from an inner voice. He said that from the time of his childhood this voice had always forbidden him to do any kind of evil. When a friend admonished him to remain silent to avoid a disagreement, Socrates said, "I cannot hold my tongue, as it would be a disobedience to a divine command."

One of his favorite doctrines was that learning is mostly remembering. He believed the doctrine that we all lived in a previous life and that the intelligence attained there influences us in this life.

Socrates was a builder of virtue, an architect of wisdom. He believed that all labor that produced courage in the mind and strength in the soul was good. He felt that he had been charged by Deity with a special mission to help people grow in godliness. He talked a great deal about the immortality of the soul. I have often thought what a thrilling event it would have been if he could have met with Jesus of Nazareth for one of the discussions he loved so much.

Socrates preceded Jesus in mortality by 470 years, but in many ways he approached Jesus about as closely as anyone. His influence and power did not come from the

27

eloquence of his words so much as from the influence of his magnificent character. Even a nod from one who is highly esteemed can have more force than a thousand arguments of studied phrases from one lacking in strength of soul.   X X X

To Socrates all wickedness was a result of either ignorance or sloth, and history seems to bear him out on this point. Had he lived in our day he would have had his work cut out for him, for he taught that the first duty of every man was to obey the law and submit to punishment when he was judged to be in error. Although most of his life was spent in teaching and reasoning, he never allowed his discussions to become heated or bitter. He always kept perfect control of himself, no matter how badly the argument went against him. Hatred had no place in his life.

When the war broke out between Athens and Sparta, Socrates enlisted and distinguished himself as a fearless warrior, excelling his fellow soldiers in the ease with which he endured hardships. He walked over the winter ice with bare feet and often pulled his belt one hole tighter in lieu of breakfast, to teach the complaining soldiers that battles could be won with discipline and endurance.

The ancient Athenians had a custom that when a commander was slain in battle, those who attended his person fought it out; if they were not victorious, then they died with their leader. Early in his life Socrates swore this same kind of allegiance to wisdom. He pledged to himself to hold wisdom and righteousness dearer than all else, and like a courageous Athenian soldier, he never thought of laying down his arms or leaving the battle before it was won.

Socrates loved to reason much as a duck loves to swim. He loved to help men discover their ignorance and understand how to correct it. He understood the truth that most men fall asleep at their posts when there

28

is no enemy in the field. It has been the fateful tendency of men to leave off thinking about a subject when the issue is no longer in doubt; when a question is definitely settled, slumber sometimes takes over. Socrates tried to keep people working and learning, for he believed that ignorance and sloth were enemies bent on destroying the uplifting pleasures of the mind. He knew that when once these spiritual joys were lost, they were difficult to recover.

Few things were more important to Socrates than his own life. He gave up his life readily when it was required of him, but he had already offered it up on the field of battle. We have every reason to believe that he was being completely honest when he said, "I care not a straw for death; my only fear is of doing some unrighteous or unholy thing." He said, "A good man ought not to calculate his chances of living or dying. He ought only to consider whether he is doing right or wrong."

Socrates never tried to make money out of his teachings. He taught because he loved wisdom and desired to develop the nobleness of others. He said, "One man finds pleasure in developing his land, another in improving his horses. But pleasure for me lies in seeing myself grow day by day." He believed that the beginning of wisdom was to understand one's own heart. In the guise of a learner he questioned the wisest men of Athens; in their answers he tried to get a reflection of his own mind. If their answers dissolved into nothingness, in the light of his reason, then his own supremacy was apparent. On the other hand, if they proved him in error, he was equally grateful and adjusted his own ideas accordingly.

Socrates' motto "Know thyself" has come down to us across the centuries as one of the wisest of counsels. He learned to know himself by watching himself. He wanted to know what he himself did when he was thwarted, crossed, contradicted, or deprived of those things that were supposed to be more desirable. He always looked upon his own mind as a kind of second party. He would try mentally to stand apart from himself and watch his own mind work. Then, should it become confused and angered, that would be proof of his insufficiency and littleness. He also watched other people and learned from them. The mixed motives that we seldom detect in our own acts can often be recognized without difficulty in someone else.

Socrates had a special cure for every defect, both in himself and in others. He accepted every fact, circumstance, and experience, and counted them all as gain. Just to live was to him a special privilege, and he included each unpleasant experience as being just as valuable as the pleasant. He believed that those who evaded unpleasant experiences were cheating themselves out of much that was worthwhile in life.

To Socrates, a good idea or an important moral principle was as much of a reality as a block of marble—and it was far more valuable. He believed that a philosopher should never speak unless his words were steeped in meaning, and that character was largely a matter of growth. As a lover of wisdom he conceived that his mission in life was to help others think and reason logically for themselves, so they would never be left at the mercy of the opinions of others. Many people came long distances to hear him. He attempted to bring about an improvement in their lives by talking them out of their ill tempers, their bad habits, and their improper attitudes. He tried to persuade others to adopt lives of simplicity and service. In his day, groups of men frequently had dinner together to discuss problems. He impressed them with the idea that at every feast two guests sit down asking for entertainment: one is the body and the other is the soul. What we give to the body it presently loses, but what we give to the soul it keeps

30

forever. At the dinners the men sat on the floor in a circle, partially leaning against each other for support. Commenting on one of the advantages of this arrangement, Socrates said that as water is made to run from a fuller to an emptier cask by means of a siphon, so wisdom flows from the greater to the less among men.

What an exciting thing it is that such a pipeline of wisdom is still in operation! The siphon of philosophy can still pour the greatness of noble men into our own lives. It can reach back 2500 years into ancient Greece and bring to us the enjoyment and profit that was generated in the lives of the men of her Golden Age.

It has been said that if Socrates had done nothing else but to give form to the mind of Plato, he would deserve the gratitude of all future centuries. Even yet it is the mind of Plato to whom thinkers turn for treasure. Plato was twenty years old and Socrates was sixty when they first met. Until Socrates died some eleven years later, they were together almost constantly. Then for the fifty years following Socrates' death, Plato recorded and expounded the wisdom of his teacher. He wanted to give all generations an insight into the brilliant mind and noble character of this unusual man.

The Storehouse of Wisdom

One of the great creations of our day is the university, an institution built for the purpose of fostering the finest kinds of human betterment. It is a place where one can go to get the knowledge, the skills, the attitudes, and the personality traits necessary to make him effective in carrying forward his part of the work of the world as well as the work of the Lord.

The university was originally set up and designed to build character and faith in its students. It fosters medical schools, experiment stations, and teaching colleges. It has libraries wherein can be found the best of culture and the greatest human thoughts that have ever been produced by the wisest men who have lived upon our earth. The purpose of the university is also to bring together teachers with fine minds and effective teaching aptitudes.

A great university is made up of schools of music, art, and science. It fosters research into fields that promote human initiative, progress, and faith. We have levied high taxes upon ourselves, and endowment funds have been accumulated, to promote universities where one can go to avail himself of the most effective occupational techniques and the finest philosophies available in our society.

In the past, many an unschooled boy worked his way through a university and came out a scientist or a teacher of culture and righteousness, or a fosterer of patriotism, idealism, and freedom. The ancient and wise Solomon said: "Wisdom is the principal thing; therefore get wisdom: and with all thy getting get understanding." (Proverbs 4:7.)

Nicholas Murray Butler, long-time president of Columbia University, once said, maybe a little facetiously, that the reason a university was sometimes referred to as a storehouse of wisdom was that the freshmen often brought more wisdom in at entrance than the seniors took out at graduation. This is certainly a very destructive possibility. It may have some application even in life itself.

Graduation time is usually a time to make an assessment of our situation and an appraisal of our future prospects. But it might be an even better idea to have our commencement exercises when we enter college rather than when we leave. By doing our thinking about it first, we may increase the chances that we will not lose too many things along the way and find ourselves worse off as seniors than we were as freshmen. In any getting process there is always a cost involved, and we pay too much of a price when we lose more values than we acquire. We must not arrive at the end of the journey with less than we had in the beginning.

Some go to college with great faith and carry away a worthless skepticism in its place. Some trade godly patriotism for satanic cynicism. Some go to college with a free mind and a wholesome spirit and leave with a whole set of damaging addictions. Some walk into a university with aspirations for marriage, a happy home, and a family of faithful children, but when they walk out they have a lot of hangups on birth control backed up by modern liberation ideas. Because of the widespread infiltration of immorality into university standards of living, some who begin college with moral purity lose it during their university experience.

During our educational period, we may make ourselves so adaptable to new ideas that we do not screen them effectively enough for their quality, beauty, or productivity, and instead of greater culture and broadened horizons of spirituality, we carry away mostly only their ashes and dust. Not only has the curriculum been invaded in many colleges and universities, but many university professors who at one time represented the finest standards of our civilization are now teaching the poisonous doctrines of communism, atheism, dishonesty, disloyalty, and immorality. It is one of the phenomena of our time that some university professors are rabidly opposed to having the name of God even mentioned in the marble halls built for us by our faithful forefathers. They seem to take delight in relieving students of their basic fundamental character traits and high spiritual values. And while some professors strenuously object to the teaching of religion, they insist on the right to teach against it.

We may be assured that those who strive to widen the breadth of today's accepted moral conduct do so to condone the evil that they themselves practice. If one vigorously derides spiritual development in others, it can be generally concluded that he has failed in that area of his own development, and he defends himself by teaching these false doctrines to others in order to make his philosophies seem acceptable. There are many who ridicule faith and spirituality, who smile in contempt when anyone mentions virtue or reverence or devotion to God or adherence to the God-given standards of morality. There are many who make their captive audiences their victims by lining up their faith, patriotism, morality, and reverence and then proceeding to riddle them with words shot out of the mouths of their own irreverence and sin.

One has a perfect right to cancel his loyalty to the church or his allegiance to the government, but normal behavior would let the matter rest at that point. However, some professors can't conduct a class without shooting barbs at those who foster spiritual interests and idealistic concepts. A part of this program of destruction is to belittle religious leaders and try and destroy the ideals they foster. There are those claiming the protection of academic freedom who are against any expression of theism by others but who insist on the right for themselves to preach atheism, which is merely the opposite side of theism. One who claims fairness should not try to destroy the one without allowing for the defense of the other.

Atheism itself is divided into many small sects, including communism, agnosticism, skepticism, humanism, and pragmatism. The atheist proclaims his own dishonesty by accepting pay to teach psychology, sociology, history, or English while he is preaching his own atheistic philosophy to his students. If the atheist wants to teach his doctrine at a public university, let him purchase property off campus and build himself a building and offer classes labeled for what they are. It should be the right of a student in any university to register for a course in English with some assurance that he will be taught the subject of English, or to register for a course in history and be taught the subject of history, and not be exposed to the distorted philosophies of an ungodly professor. If we are going to prevent the teaching of religion, we should certainly also prevent the teaching of its negative expression, atheism. Any system that protects the destruction of faith and forbids its defense must ultimately destroy the moral fiber of the people. One of the great blessings of our lives is that no one can take our values from us without our consent, but we must constantly be on guard against being seduced or led captive unaware.

We may also apply this idea to every other human experience, including life itself. We came into this life direct from the presence of God. We brought with us the blessings of a great past and a lot of wonderful future possibilities. At birth we are added upon with mortal bodies. We have been given potentially magnificent brains, and we have been endowed with personalities capable of miraculous accomplishments. We have been given the possibilities of education and occupations in which we may develop our talents. The Lord has organized his church upon the earth and given us the holy scriptures with the godly doctrines of eternal happiness and progression. But along the way we may become dropouts from education and from religion. We may throw our morality overboard and disobey God's most important commandments, which leads to failure in our primary purposes of life. Then when we come to our final graduation, before us are bodies with evil addictions, opportunities wasted, and souls condemned.

Of one group of earth's children, the Lord said, " . . . it had been better for them never to have been born." (D&C 76:32.) That is, they had spent this wonderful privilege of mortality and had less at the end than they had had at the beginning. The greatest privilege of life is to work out our own salvation in fear and trembling before God and then to be judged by our works. What a magnificent blessing it can be if we will accumulate a great volume of good works, developing godly spirits that will make us eligible to enter eternal life with many values at the end of life that we did not have at the beginning. May we make sure that we magnify our callings so that we will not lose our benefits along the way.

The Sphinx

The mythology of the ancient Greeks and Romans has many interesting stories that describe some of life's possibilities for both good and bad. One of these Greek myths is centered in the mysterious legend of the sphinx, which was supposed to be a dangerous monster. Typically it had a lion's body, a bird's wings, a human breast, and a human head.

One of the most famous of these Greek composites was the sphinx of Thebes. The Greeks had a legend that this female sphinx went around terrorizing people by demanding that they answer a riddle taught to her by the Muses. The riddle was: "What is it that has a human voice and yet becomes four-footed and two-footed and three-footed?" When the question was not answered correctly, the victim was devoured by the sphinx. Eventually, Oedipus gave the right answer, which was

"Man." The explanation of the riddle was that man ⟋
crawls on all fours in infancy, then he walks on two feet,
and finally he leans on a staff when he is old. For some
reason, when her riddle was known, the sphinx killed
herself.

Sphinx-like people have continued to operate long
after the destruction of the sphinx of Thebes. The
dictionary says that a sphinx is someone who has a
mysterious, inscrutable character, a person who deals in
enigmas that are inexplicable, puzzling, and incapable of
being understood. Such a person is one who speaks and
behaves mysteriously and is incomprehensible and
unfathomable.

To us, the ancients themselves frequently seem
puzzling and hard to understand. For example, at a great
cost in treasure, labor, and lives, they built gigantic
pyramids out in the desert of Egypt. Why those poor
people should have devoted so much of their strength to
a project of such comparative uselessness is an enigma to
us. Near the pyramids, they built the famous sphinx of
Giza in 2550 B.C. The face is a portrait of King Khafre
(Chephren) of the Fourth Dynasty, and the image is one
of the most famous monuments in all antiquity. This
sphinx, which has the recumbent body of a lion, is 172
feet along and 66 feet high; it is partly hewn from solid
sandstone and then built up with other stone.

The enigma of this sphinx is increased by the small
temple built between the lion's paws and against its
breast. No one seems certain as to what its purpose was.
I suppose that what the people did at Thebes or Giza, or
why they did it, is of small consequence to us; however,
it might remind us of some of the disadvantages to us
when we allow ourselves to become inexplicable enigmas, mysterious and incomprehensible either to ourselves or to others.

The sphinxes were always part human and part
animal. This mixing of human and animal traits did not

end when the sphinx of Giza was finished 4500 years ago. Since that time many people have been accused of resembling animals. In one of the scriptural parables, the writer of Proverbs says, "As a roaring lion, and a raging bear; so is a wicked ruler over the poor people." (Proverbs 28:15.) Peter makes an interesting comparison when he says: "Be sober, be vigilant, because your adversary the devil, as a roaring lion, walketh about, seeing whom he may devour." (1 Peter 5:8.)

Frequently we hear unhappy wives say that their husbands act like animals. The Bible refers to some men as wolves in sheep's clothing. One woman recently said that her husband was usually as cross as a bear. Since each person has different kinds of problems to contend with, many different kinds of animals may be represented in our sphinxes.

Our present-day problems, particularly in families, would not be as bad as they are if we were to build all of our unfavorable monuments out in the desert and leave them there by themselves. We add to the problem by carrying our sphinxes around with us every place we go, allowing them to expound their riddles, stir up fears, and behave so mysteriously that sometimes they cannot be understood.

Bronowski once said that "violence is the sphinx by the fireside," and then he made the significant point that "it has a human face." In this poetic metaphor he was bemoaning the fact that the violence we deplore in the world and in our own homes is not all "strange" or "criminal" or "crazy" or "bestial." Instead, like other sphinxes, violence always has a human face. The most incomprehensible sphinx of violence can be domestic and human in the most chilling sense of the word. There is an irrational human component that frequently runs through the circuits of our minds and hearts.

Contrary to what some unhappy persons may think, our major problems do not come because of the animal in man. Actually, animals do not do very many wrong things. It is the man in man that causes most of our troubles. Our grandfathers used to make a better analysis of this situation. They said that it is the devil in man that causes him to miss the mark in life.

There is little hope for any of us until we learn to recognize and control our evil tendencies. Who else but the devil or ourselves could inspire Christians to slaughter Christians in Ireland and Semites to destroy their Semite cousins in the Near East, or cause children to rebel against their parents and produce all of the human carnage that we see around us in our own land.

Our most serious wars do not take place on the battlefields of foreign lands. They are being carried on in our own homes. And our sphinxes are not always sleeping. Frequently they are fully aroused because their passions are being continually stirred and their blood is kept in a constant boil. Hate, evil, and lust for vengeance and domination too often control the centers of our thought.

Everything is evil that is not motivated by love and approved by reason. Violence may end in murder but it does not begin there. Usually violence begins quietly in a little bickering; then arguments get louder and resentments accumulate. We sometimes develop a self-centeredness that numbs our reason and destroys our love and happiness.

We are in serious trouble when the ghastly sphinx of "unrighteous dominion" takes over our lives. This sphinx begins by quietly sneaking into our lives; then, with a little success, it assumes an arrogant conviction that its sex or its position or its control of the purse strings or its might make it right. There is no appeal when one's reason has been abandoned.

Recently, a young woman, the mother of six fine children, came in to talk about some of her problems. She says that she and her husband love each other and neither of them wants a divorce. Neither of them has any other heart interest nor any record of immorality or similar wrong-doing. And yet this entire family is perfectly miserable because of her husband's sphinx that has a lust to dominate. He has an income that is far above average, but he takes the attitude that it all belongs to him personally, and he uses it as a bribe or threat to discipline the other family members. Anything he may choose to give them seems to him to be pure benevolence on his part.

When the wife wants to get the children some needed clothes, the husband maintains that she is ruining him financially. When she suggests that they sit down and talk about it, he refuses. As their money disappears each month, instead of figuring out what happened to it, he just assumes that in some mysterious way she is responsible. He is an enigma that cannot be reasoned with.

This man never questions his assumption that he is always right in everything he does and that his wife and children are always wrong. His selfishness and inability to see any other point of view except his own gives a harmful conviction to his distorted opinions, and thus he always convinces himself and seriously confuses his victims.

There are many reasons why we should try to make our sphinx have understanding and be reasonable. It is very difficult to live with an enigma who behaves mysteriously. We have a great self-training job ahead if we have a character that is inscrutable, puzzling, and inexplicable.

Just suppose someone were going to carve the image of our sphinx in stone 172 feet long and 66 feet high so that all of the details could be given. Which of the animals would be represented? We might hear some of the roaring of the lion, the screeches of the vulture, and the rampaging of the bull in the china shop. And, as Mr.

Bronowski indicates, it might have a human face—our face.

The greatest responsibility God has ever laid upon any human being is to make the most and the best of his own life. Our destiny is not to develop any animal parts or characteristics. Certainly it was not intended that we should either think or act like the devil. Each one of us was created in God's own image, and each of us has been endowed with his attributes and potentialities, the development of which is one of the purposes for which we live.

We should cling to our inheritance and be constantly reaffirming it in our lives, for each of us is truly a child of God. Instead of being inexplicable and incapable of being understood, our lives should be an open book so that everyone, including ourselves, can read an inspiring chapter on every contact.

Repentance is one of the first and most important principles of the gospel. Like Mary of Magdala, most of us have a few devils that need to be cast out. James said, "Resist the devil, and he will flee from thee." (James 4:7.) On the other hand, Jesus said: "Follow me." We can follow him in his reason, in his goodness, and in his faith. Then the image of us will have the form of a magnificent human being with a godly soul and a godly personality, and a godly face—our face.

The Happy Prince

Many years ago, Oscar Wilde wrote a fantasy of a fine young man whom he called "The Happy Prince." During his lifetime this young man lived in a royal palace with high walls enclosing beautiful grounds. The walls

41

excluded much of the ugliness and misery of the outside world. Most of the daily activities of the prince were made up of joys because of his pleasant activities, and so he was called the Happy Prince. At his death a beautiful statue was made in his likeness and placed on top of a tall column high above the city.

The statue was not only very beautiful, but it also cost a great deal of money. A large red ruby was mounted in the handle of the sword that hung at the prince's side. The Happy Prince's eyes were represented by two beautiful sapphires from India. His uniform was made of hundreds of leaves of pure gold. As the statue stood there on its pedestal above the city, it shone and glistened in the sunlight and all the people looked up and admired it. They loved it because of the happiness that had characterized the prince's life.

Then one day a little swallow, belated in its flight for its winter rest in the warm sun of Egypt, flew up to the monument of the Happy Prince to spend the night between the prince's feet. As he was about to tuck his head under his wing, a large drop of water fell upon him. The swallow looked up and saw that the eyes of the Happy Prince were filled with tears. The Happy Prince explained that because he had been placed high above the city, he was saddened by the misery, poverty, suffering, and sin he could clearly see all about him. The swallow was thinking only of a good night's rest so he could continue his journey; however, the Happy Prince entreated him to stay a few days and be his messenger.

The prince pointed out to the little swallow the abode of a poor seamstress living in dingy rooms across the roofs of the city. She worked night and day at her sewing, trying to get enough money to provide for her sick son who was tossing in his bed close by with a burning fever. The prince persuaded the little swallow to take the ruby out of his sword hilt and give it to the tired mother. This deed of generosity and kindness caused great happiness to the seamstress and brought relief from suffering to her son.

As the swallow was making some of his trips over the city, he saw the cathedral spires and watched the workmen carry out their various assignments of toil, and he and the Happy Prince discussed the many cases of misery and need that lay all about them. Then the prince asked the swallow to pluck out one of his sapphire eyes and give it to a young man living in a garret who could not work because of the bitter cold. They saw a poor little match girl who had allowed her matches to get wet and who was afraid to go home because her father would mistreat her. The Happy Prince begged the swallow to take his other eye so that the little match girl could take something home to her father and she would not be punished.

The Happy Prince was now completely blind, so he persuaded his dear friend and messenger to fly over the city and tell him what he saw. As each case came up that needed help, the Happy Prince would order the little swallow to pick off some of his golden leaves and carry them to those who were in need. With the little swallow serving as the messenger of the Happy Prince, light came into children's faces, hungry people were fed, and sick people were made well.

At intervals the little swallow would think about his friends who were waiting for him in Egypt, but he could not leave the prince in his attempts to bring joy to other people. But finally all of the golden leaves were gone, and the prince no longer lighted the city with his brilliant reflection. The mayor and his councilmen looked up and remarked how drab and shabby the statue had become. Their hero now looked no better than a beggar, so they decided that his statue must be taken down. The workmen discovered that the lead heart of the Happy Prince had broken, and they found a dead swallow lying beneath the prince's feet.

It may be that as Oscar Wilde was writing this story, he was thinking of that scriptural passage which says, ". . . none of us liveth to himself, and no man dieth to himself." (Romans 14:7.)

All mankind were created to live together in nations and in families, and to work together for the good of all. There was a period following the time of Christ when the record said, ". . . they had all things common. . . . Neither was there any among them that lacked." (Acts 4:32, 34.)

However, it seems that we have not been good enough to maintain this standard for a very long period at a time, so the Lord has replaced it with the law of tithing and other welfare programs. These have many advantages, because a large group of people can help solve the problems of individuals much more easily than a few having such limited resources as those possessed by the Happy Prince and the swallow.

All of us seem to be beggars in many ways. We are dependent upon God and other people, and God has conditioned what we receive from him by what we give to others who are in need. It is a divine scriptural law that with what measure we mete, it shall be measured unto us again. (See Matthew 7:2.) Jesus said, "Give, and it shall be given unto you; good measure, pressed down, and shaken together, and running over, shall men give into your bosom." (Luke 6:38.)

For a number of years Peter Marshall served as chaplain of the United States Senate. One morning in his opening prayer he said to the Lord: "Make us a part of the answer and not a part of the problem." Too frequently we ourselves cause serious problems that unnecessarily consume the efforts of other people. It would take a good many Happy Prince and little swallow combinations to supply the damaging thirsts of alcoholics, dope addicts, moral perverts, and those who rebel against God. The greatest responsibility of every human being is to take care of himself, and the first soul that anyone should bring to God is his own soul.

President Franklin D. Roosevelt once recited an old Chinese prayer, which said, "Reform the world, and start with me." Handling our own problems is a job no one can do quite as well as we ourselves can.

We should also devote some of our time to helping others. The Happy Prince gave his ideas and his substance and himself to help others, and we should do the same. Each of us has many things to give. We can give encouragement, love, enthusiasm, ideas, and our substance.

Frequently as I have flown over a large city, I have looked down and seen the millions of lights that represent individual human families, all of whom probably have problems with which they need help. However, my vision is limited from that distance, and like the Happy Prince with no eyes, I cannot see these important human needs. But in our ordinary contacts we usually have a closer view where we can see into the lives of people, and feel their suffering and despair.

I have thought of God, who is also located high above the city. The scriptures tell that of all the things upon the earth, nothing is hidden from him. He understands our miseries as well as our joys, and he even understands all of our thoughts that lead to them. I can imagine that he may sometimes become very sad when he sees those wrong things that we do. A lot of evils take place every day that would tend to break his heart. It is certain that all of the problems and miseries of the world could be avoided if everyone strictly kept his commandments.

Under the universal law of free agency, God has done about as much as he can for our benefit and happiness until we do something for ourselves. He has organized his church. He has taught the principles of the gospel. He has told us how to qualify for the celestial

45

kingdom. He has given us a program for taking care of those in material need. We may wipe every transgression out of our lives by our repentance. The Lord has given us the gift of the atonement and has promised us a glorious resurrection with the possibility of eternal progression and eternal increase. The scripture refers to him as the Prince of peace, and his benefits are far more valuable than rubies and sapphires and leaves of gold. He is also the Prince of righteousness, and by our righteousness we can also make him the Happy Prince. As he has been our greatest benefactor, he expects us to serve and uplift each other. If we do so, we will also be happy. Our lives are given to us that we may enjoy them. This joy can best be brought about when we are effectively engaged in the service of each other.

The Wizard of Oz

Many years ago Frank Baum wrote an interesting fantasy entitled *The Wizard of Oz*, which also has some interesting lessons to teach. The story tells of an intelligent, personable girl named Dorothy who lived on the prairies of Kansas with her Aunt Em and Uncle Henry and Toto, her dog. Her interesting experiences began when one day the cyclones for which Kansas is famous picked up the house with Dorothy and Toto in it and transported it to the magic land of Oz, where she landed among the friendly Munchkins. She immediately became a heroine because her house dropped upon and killed the Wicked Witch of the West, an enemy of the Munchkins.

Dorothy and Toto were very anxious to get back to Aunt Em and Uncle Henry in Kansas, so the Munchkins suggested that she should go to Emerald City and consult the Wizard of Oz about her problem.

In her journey along the yellow brick road leading to Emerald City, Dorothy had many interesting experiences. She came upon a scarecrow who was having trouble because he was losing too much of his straw stuffing. Being a friendly, helpful person, Dorothy stopped and stuffed his straw back into him where it belonged. She told the scarecrow of her own problem of getting back to Kansas and that she was hopeful the Wizard of Oz might be able to help her. In turn, the scarecrow unburdened himself to Dorothy and told her of his life-long desire to possess a brain instead of the meager straw that had been stuffed into his head. They agreed that if the Wizard could get Dorothy and Toto back to Kansas, he might also be able to help the scarecrow to get a brain.

After they had proceeded for a time down the road together they met a tin woodman, whose job was to cut down trees with his ax. However, a recent rain had caused his tin to rust, and his joints were so stiff that he could not move. He told Dorothy there was an oil can close by, and she obligingly oiled his joints so he was again able to move. The tin woodman told his new friends of his desire to have a heart, and everyone agreed that the best solution would be for them all to seek the aid of the Wizard of Oz.

Finally in their journey they met a cowardly lion. All of the lion's friends were supposed to look up to him as the king of the beasts; by tradition he was the master of the jungle. But he was very unhappy because his feelings of inadequacy caused serious cowardice. And so the cowardly lion also joined the company in seeking the help of the Wizard of Oz.

Upon their arrival at the Emerald City, they were opposed by the Witch of the East. They also discovered that the Wizard of Oz was not a wizard at all. After he had been exposed, he admitted that he was a humbug.

But he did convince the scarecrow that everyone can have a brain who can learn to use one. He then gave the scarecrow a diploma so he could prove to himself and to everyone else he had a brain and could think. The Wizard put a chain around the tin woodman's neck with a golden heart on it, showing that he had a heart and all he had to do was to learn how to use it. He gave the cowardly lion a medal proving primarily to the lion himself that he had valor and courage. The Wizard of Oz was a humbug, and yet he was also a wizard.

Dorothy had made friends with a good fairy, who told her and her companions that all of them could have anything they wanted if only they wanted it hard enough. She told them how to want and wish with greater power. Consequently, Dorothy's friends soon had what they wanted, and it wasn't very long before Toto and Dorothy themselves were back with Aunt Em and Uncle Henry in Kansas.

Like Dorothy and her friends, we all have important journeys to make down that yellow brick road of life. In addition, we all have need for many of the same things. Everyone is in need of a better brain than that handful of straw that is under so many hats.

Someone has asked this question: "How would you like to create your own mind?" But isn't that exactly what we do? William James said, "The mind is made up by what it feeds upon." The mind, like the dyer's hand, is colored by what it holds. If I hold in my hand a sponge full of purple dye, my hand becomes purple. If I hold in my mind and heart some great ideas, my whole personality is colored accordingly. If we want to have strong minds, we ought to use them a lot and feed them on the right things. Brains are not only inherited, but like our muscles they are also developed by effective use. At some time in our lives most of us feel like we have some variety of straw brains.

Woodrow Wilson said, "The greatest ability of the

American people is their ability to resist instruction." Most of us have our share of that unfortunate talent. Thomas A. Edison once said that there is nothing a man wouldn't do to avoid thinking. For some people, thinking is the most disagreeable, unpleasant, boring employment they ever have. And yet Solomon said, "As a man thinketh in his heart, so is he." (Proverbs 23:7.) Now, I don't know just where that leaves us, but if we are what we think and if we don't think, then it becomes pretty evident that we have a problem.

Someone once voiced a great success idea when he said: "Us guys that ain't got no education has got to use our brains." If we don't want to be straw men, we need to develop our brains. What a thrill that we can feed our minds on the greatest ideas of industry, enthusiasm, faith, decision making, and action taking.

It is also very important, as we make our way toward that magical city in our own lives, that we discover and develop some finer, warmer heart qualities. Our emotions sometimes get a little bit rusty so that our joints don't move very well. Frank Baum's tin woodman wanted to feel the emotions of excitement and love running through his system. How difficult it is for one to go through his life without a heart; then it is impossible for him to fall in love with life or with the great world of wonders in which he lives. Some people can't fall in love with their families or with righteousness or with God. Heart exercises are among the things that make life worthwhile, and yet, like the tin woodman, many people go through their lives with rusty joints.

Some time ago I saw a man who didn't have any hands. There are many other people who do have hands but don't know how to use them. Some people have idle hands, some have lazy hands, some have unfriendly hands, and some have ignorant, unskilled hands. And while we are visiting with our Wizard of Oz, it may be that he could fix us up with a pair of friendly, willing, enthusiastic hands that could move mountains or save souls or more effectively greet our friends.

In Mr. Baum's story the lion also had a difficult situation. He was born to be the king of beasts, and what a tragedy that somewhere along the way he had lost his courage. As a consequence of losing his courage, he had also lost his composure and his self-confidence. In the real drama of life we must not lose our courage or our kingship.

We all need brains that are not made of straw; oil on our joints so we can move around and use the great powers of our hearts; and the courage and willingness to perform miracles. As the good fairy said to Dorothy and her friends, "If we want anything enough, we may obtain it."

Thanks, King

One of the emotions that we have a common interest in is the emotion of gratitude. We are all indebted to God for life and all its benefits. Gratitude is a parent ability; it brings forth after its own kind. Cicero, the Roman statesman, once said that gratitude was the mother of virtues.

Gratitude implies affection and love. The gratitude one feels for his country, his parents, his children, and for God all differ widely at different times, but all are based on love. If someone does a small courtesy for us we may give them a sincere "thank you." When they do some greater service, we may have trouble expanding our words to match the increased benefit received. If we would give someone a small but sincere thank you for a friendly greeting or a kind deed, how would we thank

God for life and an everlasting opportunity and eternal happiness?

We have a memorable lesson in gratitude given us by the Indian boy Jim Thorpe, who was born in 1888. He grew up on the plains of Oklahoma. In 1911 he attended the small Carlisle University, where he became a great athlete under the stimulating direction of a young coach named Pop Warner. In 1912, Jim participated in the Olympic Games in Sweden and was by far the outstanding performer. After the games he was given a royal banquet by King Gustav of Sweden, but because of Jim's weakness for liquor, he was unable to attend the banquet. King Gustav himself presented Jim Thorpe with a gold medal, and Jim also received a life-size bronze bust of the king. In an elaborate presentation speech, the king said to this young Indian boy, "Sir, you are the greatest athlete in the world." In accepting the bust, the medals, and the other honors and expressions of appreciation and kindnesses extended to him by the king himself, his host country, and its royal family, Jim gave his own expression of appreciation in his famous response: "Thanks, King."

Following this historic event, he had a great deal of trouble because he had accepted some money for playing a few games of summer baseball and thus was guilty of a technical violation of his amateur athletic standing. Therefore, he was asked by the Olympic committee to return his medals, which themselves had an intrinsic value of over $50,000.

Because of reversals in his fortunes, caused by his own weaknesses and bad habits, great bitterness grew up in Jim's heart. His weaknesses destroyed most of the advantages his earlier excellence had given him.

However, all through his life Jim remembered what the king had said about his being the greatest athlete in the world, and nothing could take those words away from him. Although he lived and died in poverty and

51

trouble, he was always enriched by the memory of the king's words, "Sir, you are the greatest athlete in the world."

Jim Thorpe came to Carlisle University a skinny youngster weighing 130 pounds. During his college period he turned himself into 185 pounds of muscle, strong ligaments, split-second reflexes, and a keen competitive brain that gave him supremacy in football and track and every other sport in which he engaged. In football he was a brilliant ball carrier, a fine blocker and passer, an excellent receiver, and the game's greatest all-around kicker. He rated the All-American halfback designation in 1911 and 1912. During his junior year, Lafayette University played host to Carlisle in a track meet, during which Jim racked up practically every blue ribbon on the field. Singlehandedly he routed the entire Lafayette track team.

Carlisle played Brown University on Thanksgiving day in 1912. The referee said that all by himself, Jim Thorpe defeated the entire Brown University by a score of 32 to 0. In 1912 he was the decathlon and pentathlon winner at the Olympics in Stockholm. On February 11, 1950, an Associated Press Dispatch from New York carried a headline that stated: "Thorpe Named Top Athlete." The article said, "Jim Thorpe, the almost legendary figure of the sports world, had additional laurels heaped upon his leathern brow Saturday when the nation's sports experts named him the greatest athlete of this half century." Thorpe had previously been voted the number one football player of the past fifty years; he also became the only double winner in the Associated Press poll when 252 out of 393 sports writers and radio broadcasters accorded him this honor. In order, the first three places were voted as follows: Thorpe, 252; Babe Ruth, 86; and Jack Dempsey, 19.

Just think what might have happened if Jim Thorpe had been able to maintain that training and excellence throughout his life. However, because of liquor and other personal problems, his later years were bitter. He brooded a great deal. He was unable to maintain himself for long in any occupation that was remunerative or satisfying to him. He soon dropped from sight, and not much was heard of him again until his death on March 27, 1953, at age 64, in a trailer house outside Los Angeles.

When we come into the world, most of us are given advantages of body, mind, home, and teaching. If we could just learn and practice gratitude and appreciation and respond in kind, our lives would be happier and more successful. But sometimes those with the greatest possibilities deny their own future with ingratitude. We sometimes break our parents' hearts or set a bad example for our associates. Some become disloyal to their country, rebel against the finest social traditions, and fight the establishment. Frequently those who ought to be the most grateful disown their responsibilities and even fight against God. Usually they also become bitter, resentful, and unhappy. We ought not to waste even one precious day of this life in bitterness or ingratitude. Jim Thorpe had a wonderful body, a keen mind, and a fine spirit. But on the very brink of what could have been a magnificent accomplishment, he let weaknesses get in his way, and a great possible future career went down the drain.

What about us? For our manifold blessings, everyone in the world ought to look up toward heaven and say, "Thanks, God. Thanks for everything." Then we could make a firm pledge to him that we would never break the rules of the game nor violate any of the laws made to govern our eternal success.

The accolade that Jim Thorpe received from King Gustav was wonderful, but the King of kings has pointed out that a straight and narrow way leads to life, and only he who endures to the end shall be saved.

2
DEVELOPING OUR PERSONALITIES WITH WISDOM

"Wisdom is the principal thing;
therefore get wisdom: and with all
thy wisdom get understanding."

Wisdom Is the Principal Thing

There has been a great deal of discussion over the years on what is the greatest good. Henry Drummond wrote a stimulating essay entitled "The Greatest Thing in the World." His argument is based on the inspiring thirteenth chapter of First Corinthians, one of the masterpieces of our literature, in which Paul says, "And now abideth faith, hope, charity, these three; but the greatest of these is charity." Jesus pointed out two aspects of this important idea when he said we should love God with all of our hearts and our neighbors as ourselves.

Solomon said, "Wisdom is the principal thing; therefore get wisdom: and with all thy getting get understanding." (Proverbs 4:7.) Try to imagine what a society we would have if each of us always exercised good judgment, if we were always wise in our choices, if we thoroughly understood each situation so that our wisdom could be fully depended upon. We sometimes give credit for greatness to chance or those circumstances and influences that were in our heredity antedating our birth. We sometimes say that a person is a natural-born salesman or a natural-born teacher or a natural-born golfer. Everyone has at least two personalities, the one that he is born with and the one he acquires after he is born. It is the acquired personality that we use in becoming a successful teacher, businessman, scientist, or husband or wife. The principal ingredient in all of these successes is the element of being wise in what we do.

Just as nothing is born fully grown, so no one begins his life with a head full of knowledge or muscles filled with skills and self-control or a nervous system ripened with stability. We learn how to be good husbands and bank presidents just as we learn to be expert basketball players, golfers, and skaters. Each of us begins his life with great possibilities, and where we go from there is up to us.

With the right kind of study and labor and with a few other things added in, each of us may develop wisdom and good judgment. Certainly we ought to explore the possibilities of more effectively cultivating these important qualities for our own lives.

Wisdom is the quality of being able to judge sincerely and deal sagaciously with facts, especially as they relate to life and conduct. It is the capacity to make the best use of knowledge. It involves the ability to make the best use of time and opportunity. It is the proper development of talent. It is a perception not only of the best ends, but also of the best means. It is the ability to use practical know-how. It adds excellence to our lives.

And so we might adopt as a theme and goal for our lives the statement of the wise man Solomon, who said, "Wisdom is the principal thing; therefore get wisdom: and with all thy getting get understanding." We should work on this project as though our life depended upon it, as indeed it does.

Basic Character

The kind of character we develop determines on which end of the success scale our lives belong. There is a great similarity between physical structure and our character structure, for as the bony skeleton gives us physical strength and power, so our basic character furnishes us the power to reach our divine destiny.

God himself has developed a perfect character, one that not only knows right from wrong, but one that is also dedicated irrevocably to right and is set in eternal opposition to wrong. God cannot look upon sin with the least degree of allowance. His strong commitments and his unchangeable nature make it impossible for him to fail, for he is the same yesterday, today, and forever. It is this basic, unchangeable, righteous character that makes God God, and we should train ourselves to follow his example. It is important for us to develop a strong physical backbone with its some two hundred other supporting bones, but it is even more important that we develop moral backbone composed of a righteous human character. The general benefits that we receive from a good character guarantee to us every other success and happiness.

The Boy Scout organization attempts to build this kind of character into its members. Before any boy is permitted to have even a Tenderfoot membership in the Scout organization, he must make a solemn pledge: "On my honor I will do my best to do my duty to God and my country and to obey the Scout Law; to help other people at all times; to keep myself physically strong, mentally awake and morally straight." These sacred pledges, if lived, would constitute a godly strengthening in the skeleton of each participating boy.

The first part of this pledge has to do with performing one's duty to God and country. The second has to do with maintaining a high relationship of genuine service to others, and in the third, each boy makes a solemn pledge to himself of physical cleanliness, intellectual excellence, and moral righteousness. Then he attempts to develop within himself those laws of righteousness centered in the following twelve basic character principles:

1. Trustworthiness
2. Loyalty
3. Helpfulness
4. Friendliness

5. Courtesy
6. Kindness
7. Obedience
8. Cheerfulness
9. Thrift
10. Bravery
11. Cleanliness
12. Reverence

When we refer to character by itself without any qualifying adjectives, we automatically imply a good character. Yet our world is full of people who lack character or who have some negative character traits. Evil character traits are fathered by Satan. The dictionary says that character is the aggregate of distinctive mental and moral qualities belonging to an individual or to mankind as a whole. A man's character is what he is. His reputation is what others think he is. One is the substance, the other is the shadow. Emerson said that character ranks higher than intellect. It must stand behind and back up every other thing. Character is a moral vigor or skeletal firmness that we acquire through self-discipline, and our individual traits serve as the index to our essential or intrinsic value.

In recent years, we have been made aware of a serious worsening taking place in the world that forms an unusual contrast with the brighter background of our earlier history. This consists primarily of processes that are eroding away fundamental character qualities. In many places honor is being replaced with dishonor; truth is not as valuable as it once was; delinquency and criminal activities have increased enormously. In the past men lived by the inspiring old axiom that an honest man is the noblest work of God. Yet, to many people today, lying and deception have become a way of life. We have torn down the pedestals from which our earlier heroes lifted us upward. We do not have the same kind of confidence in our great educational institutions that we formerly did, and many students have become rebels, vandals, and fosterers of immorality. Probably more important than all of these other downward trends is that so many people deny their responsibilities as children of God.

Recently a woman came to talk with me about her problems. She and her husband have six young children. The husband was immoral before they were married, and he has had several immoral affairs during their marriage. He has made many pledges to his wife and children, promising them one day a happy, united, righteous family life, and yet the next day disappearing for several days without anyone knowing where he is. Though he is immoral and irresponsible, he is a teacher in the public schools. He makes contributions to the financial welfare of the family only if it pleases him to do so, but he is not dependable as a means of family support. His wife works two eight-hour shifts each day, and from her two incomes she supports their six children; yet he accuses her of being a poor housekeeper. The children love their father; yet they plead with their mother to divorce him. This man, a college graduate, forces his wife and children to undergo the torments of hell merely because he is irresponsible and lacks those fundamentals of basic character that should identify him as a man. He might be described as a mental and spiritual jellyfish who has no moral backbone or strong personal commitments to manhood. His occasional impulses toward righteousness cause him to make promises, and then the weakness of his undisciplined will prevents them from being fulfilled.

Someone has said: "He who acts wickedly in private life can never be expected to show himself noble in public conduct. He who is base at home will not acquit himself with honor abroad; for it is not the man, but only the place that is changed." In contrast to this gloomy picture, we might think of God himself, who never wavers or vacillates. He is always the same.

Colton has said that anyone should be willing to give twenty thousand pounds for a good character because he could immediately make double that sum by its use. When J. P. Morgan was asked what he considered the best bank collateral, he replied "Character." The best characters are formed by vigorous and persistent resistance to evil tendencies. No one can wish or dream himself into a good character. He must hammer and forge one for himself. Lloyd George said: "There is nothing so fatal to character as half-finished tasks." J. J. Gurney has added: "A tree will not only lie as it falls, but it will fall as it leans."

The beast was placed down on all fours and thus his vision is cast upon the ground, but man was created upright in the image of his Maker, so that he might look up to God. Solomon said: "With all thy getting, get understanding." (Proverbs 4:7.) And we might reassert our central purpose by adding: "With all thy getting, get character."

Our Moods

One of the great powers operating in our lives is called emotion. Each person has a collection of these mysterious forces, which are capable of taking him either backward or forward or up or down.

In his first inaugural address, U.S. President Dwight D. Eisenhower said that the great driving forces of the world were not intellectual but emotional. Enormous power is generated by what and how we think and feel.

Moods vary widely. One may have a sullen or morose state of mind. A bad temper or anger may lead to arrogance or cruelty. Sin causes a particular low tide in our mood and leaves us vulnerable to all kinds of temptations. If we allow ourselves to be moody, we may go in the wrong direction, since many of the powerful moods are caused by hate, anger, selfishness, negative thinking, and fear.

However, moods are not all bad, for our emotions can carry us up as well as down. There are certain things that bring on joyful, happy moods and cause a general elevation of our lives. Shakespeare even speaks of a beneficial fear, which he calls the fear that reason leads. Our fears can be helpful if we are afraid of the right things at the right time. President James A. Garfield once said, "I am afraid of doing any evil thing." When we develop enough fear of ignorance, sin, unfairness, dishonesty, weakness, and failure, we set in motion uplifting moods. We should see to it that our moods include the powerful motivating factors of reason, ambition, and good judgment. We should determine in our minds what our objectives are and ought to be and then run up a full emotional sail in such a way that the power of our moods and feelings can carry us to our destination.

Ralph Waldo Emerson once said that in his personal life, the thing he needed most was for someone who could get him to do those things that he already knew he ought to do. That is, he needed the emotional power to put in force those things that his reason and good judgment told him should be done. He explained that one of his difficulties came because he could not get his moods to believe in each other.

The main business of Mr. Emerson's life was thinking and writing. Sometimes he was deluged by a rush of ideas, and he could not write fast enough to get them down on paper before they vanished. At such a time, he could never imagine that this wonderful high tide in his thinking would ever change. He compared this situation to the maple syrup harvest in New England in the spring. There were times when the sap would flow from the maple trees in such abundance that it would overflow all containers placed there to gather the syrup, and those in charge could not bring new containers fast enough.

Then Mr. Emerson's mood would change. He would lose the spirit. He said that he could not write very well with his pen in one hand while he had a peat knife or a crowbar in the other. When his negative thinking overcame his enthusiasm, he would find himself in a devastating mental low tide from which he had great difficulty recovering. At such times the gift of the happy phrase refused to come. Then it was as though the maple trees of his brain were completely dead, and that no matter what he did, his imagination refused to work. He would be taken over by discouragement and despair and obsessed with fear and unhappiness. Most important of all, he could not get himself to believe that this situation would ever change.

However, he discovered that if he kept constantly at work, studying, thinking, and writing, and excluding from his mind all neutralized emotions or antagonistic thoughts, it would not be long before the drought season would pass and the mental syrup would again be overflowing. His ideas would again be like a great cloud of intellectual butterflies trying to light on his brain.

This contrast of emotional feasts and famine is one of the problems of every life, and one of the important secrets of success is how to cure our destructive moods before they take place. We do ourselves great damage when we sin at night and then hate ourselves in the morning. The addict is all enthused about getting high on drugs this week, and then he spends next week in contemplating suicide. After every sin of gluttony, some of us firmly make up our minds that we will eat nothing more for the rest of the week, but before the next mealtime has arrived, our mood has changed and we are ready to reindulge. Our moods not only disbelieve each other, but are actually hostile and destructive.

Some time ago, as I walked down the street, I stopped for a few minutes to admire the beautiful display in the window of a candy store. In a communication that was stronger than any words, my stomach urged me, "Go in and get the candy." However, my brain, which is always concerned with my best interests, immediately got into the discussion and advised me not to get the candy. Then it gave me a dozen reasons why I shouldn't get the candy. Number one, it said, "You've already had your lunch." Number two, "You're not particularly undernourished." Number three, "You already have a problem of several pounds of excess baggage." Number four, "If you get the candy, your problem will be increased, you won't look as well, you won't be able to work as hard, your willpower will be lessened for the next showdown, further jeopardy will be placed on your health, and your indulgence is expensive and solves nothing. In fact, eating always increases your appetite." I carefully considered these reasons and found every one of them to be absolutely true. Never in my lifetime, when my brain has had the right information, has it ever tried to deceive me, while my stomach is always urging me to do things against my own interests. I went over these reasons with my stomach, and said, "How are you going to answer this logic?" But my stomach never reasons at all—it just urges. It kept saying, "Go in and get the candy."

I always try to be reasonable and fair and give full consideration to both sides of an argument, but after considering both sides I went in and got the candy. This is not the first time that I have sided with my stomach against my brain. And my brain gets a little demoralized, for it knows that it was appointed to be the presiding officer of my personality. Everything I do is supposed to be checked and approved by my brain, and my brain sometimes becomes confused because it knows from past experience that no matter how reasonable its directions may be, it cannot always depend that I will follow its logic.

I often have conflict going on between my brain and my stomach, even though my brain is very intelligent and my stomach is devoid of all reasoning power. I have discovered that it is easy for one to get into the habit of thinking with his appetites.

Sometimes we let our moods place our wills in slavery. Powerful appetites that we allow to get control over us can make even the most heinous sin seem pleasant at the moment, but after the passion is past and the sin has been committed, we tend to be sorry for what we have done and our mood changes to miserable regret. But this so-called repentance may not last long, and soon we are ready to turn back to our wallow.

Someone said of a man who was trying to establish spirituality in his life that he wore out the knees of his trousers in trying to get religion and then he wore out the seat of his pants in backsliding. Many people go through a literal hell in suffering ups and downs as the conflicts of their moods continue. What we need is a stronger central control of our lives. We need to make up our minds what is right and what is wrong and where we want to go, and then get a powerful set of positive emotions to take us there.

There are many arguments against gluttony and obesity, and the arguments are just as valid while we are eating as they are immediately after we have finished. The arguments against immorality should be just as convincing to us when the temptation is present as they are after shame and regret have destroyed our happiness and peace of mind. Someday everyone will stand before God. No one will then want to be an atheist or a weakling or a telestial personage. Everyone will believe in God during the final judgment, and everyone will then want to be a devoted, enthusiastic, whole-souled member of God's celestial kingdom. It is a pretty good idea for us to repent before the deed is committed and to make our pledge against our sins before the damage has all been done.

The magnificent brains with which we have been endowed are much more effective to think with than are our stomachs or our hates or our sex urges or any feelings of support that we have for doing wrong. We need to set our goals by the scriptures and by listening to the dictates of our spirits and the logic of our brains, and then get our emotions for righteousness behind us to push us toward the place where we would someday like to be.

Imagination

The most complicated piece of machinery in the world is a human being. We have seen the automobile, the radio, the television, and other inventions in their beginnings as very crude instruments, and then we have watched them evolve to their present place of comparative excellence. But each human being easily qualifies as the greatest invention God himself has ever devised. From the very beginning man has been loaded with potential miracles and wonders that even he himself cannot begin to understand.

Someone has said that the greatest gift God has given to man is an imagination. With an imagination we can go forward or backward across time or space with greater facility than we could get across the street. With an active imagination we can relive the past and we can pre-live the future. In *Gospel Ideals*, President David O.

McKay has a paragraph in which he said: "Last night I dreamed about my mother." And then he said: "I would like to dream about my mother more often." President McKay did not learn those lessons of life that brought him to his ultimate high place when he was fifty or sixty or seventy. He learned them at five, ten, and fifteen at his mother's knee; then, in his later years, he was able to go back in his dreams and relive the experiences with his mother while he reabsorbed the original good.

Each person may regularly go back and relive his marriage vows or the covenants he made at the waters of baptism. We can relive crises in our lives when we promised God that under all circumstances we would be faithful. Or we may go in the other direction looking toward the future, so that a young person can pre-live his marriage and discover the qualities that he would like to establish in himself before that important occasion arrives. In a similar way, we may pre-live our death or go across the boundaries of mortality and pre-live our own eternal life.

We may learn to form mental images, to pre-live experiences, to project answers, and to make decisions, even before a problem has arisen. Before an architect erects a building of steel, concrete, and glass, he constructs an image in his mind and then puts it down on paper. When Orville Wright was a little boy he asked his father, "Can a man fly?" Then for hours at a time he and his brother, Wilbur, would lie on their backs watching the birds fly overhead. They discussed such questions as this: "If birds and bees could fly, why couldn't men?" They wondered how the billions of tons of rainwater were carried across the sky to refresh the thirsty ground. It was inevitable, with enough imagination, that they would eventually make their famous sixty-second flight in Kittyhawk, North Carolina, to start the air age on its way.

The imagination has the power to disassemble its

component parts and then recombine the various elements in any of thousands of combinations to bring about any result. The dictionary says that imagination is the act, process, or power to form mental images that are not actually present, a mental synthesis of new ideas from elements that have been experienced separately.

Many years ago H. G. Wells wrote an interesting fantasy about a man who invented a machine in which he could travel through time, much as we now travel through space. He could go thousands of years into the future in a period of just a few minutes, and the speedometer of the time machine always indicated which year of time he was in. He could study peoples, civilizations, the institutions as they would some day actually be. Then he would get back into his time machine and return to the present.

By pushing the lever in the other direction, the scientist could with equal speed go back into the past. Being a historian, he took delight in witnessing the important events of history while they were actually taking place. He could personally verify the account of the Battle of Hastings by going back to the year 1066. By going still further back, he could visit the Golden Age of Greece to 400 B.C., and personally discuss philosophy with Socrates.

This philosophy is much more than a fantasy. God has given a kind of time-traveling ability to the prophets. For example, he took Abraham back into his own antemortal existence and let him experience conditions as they existed when he lived with God and walked by sight. John the Revelator pushed the lever in the other direction, and from his lonely exile on the Isle of Patmos near the end of the first century he went forward past the end of our world as we know it to the time of the final judgment. In telling us of this experience, he said, "And I saw the dead, small and great, stand before God; and the books were opened: and another book was opened, which is the book of life: and the dead were judged out of those things which were written in the books, according to their works." (Revelation 20:12.)

An imagination not only has the power to take us backward or forward; it can also take us up or down. The mind is equipped with the power to dream great dreams of accomplishment. Just a few years ago we were dreaming dreams of flying carpets and seven league boots and magic wishing caps and Aladdin lanterns. We have already made these dreams out of date because we have so far surpassed them all.

Abraham Lincoln once said that any man can be about as happy as he makes up his mind to be. We can also be about as wise as we make up our minds to be. Our minds can take us to the very gates of exaltation or they can cast us down to the lowest levels of despondency, depression, and even hell itself. We do not know the extent a mind can go in making us miserable.

But our minds were not given us to damn us. They were given to help us bring about better conditions of happiness. And so we push the lever up while we live life at its best and as it ought to be lived. The first step to any accomplishment is to believe in it.

As the little girl plays mother to her dolls, she is building the roadway for her own future. Boys who play at being gangsters will be different kinds of men from those who imagine themselves to be patriots. Those whose industry places them in the center of accomplishment will rise above those who revel in idleness, drunkenness, and sin. We become what we think.

All we have to do to have the most magnificent castles in the air is to learn how to put some good mental foundations under them. However, we should carefully control the thinking power of our imagination. Otherwise it can take us where we don't want to go or turn us into something we don't want to be.

The chief purpose of this life is to prepare us for something better. It is a probationary state, a period of testing, of proving, of aspiring and developing. We aspire in secret and it comes to pass. There is no other objective in the world so worthy of the full power of our imagination as the celestial kingdom. As we read the words of the prophets and understand the eternal principles of progress, we can get into the time machines of our minds and pre-live the details of our destiny. May God help us to fully pre-live our possibilities.

Blessed Are the Peacemakers

The greatest sermon ever preached is known to us as the Sermon on the Mount. In this discourse Jesus refers to nine conditions of blessedness, or Beatitudes, that he desired that we should strive to attain. In one of these Beatitudes, he said, "Blessed are the peacemakers, for they shall be called the children of God." (Matthew 5:9.)

The dictionary gives a number of definitions for the word *peace*. It says that peace is a state of tranquillity, freedom from disturbance, a lack of agitation. It is a state of being free from war and other forms of hostility. Peace describes harmony in personal relationships. It is the mutual concord or amity that exists between people.

Peace is a mental or spiritual state in which there is freedom from all disquieting and disturbing influences. To make peace is to agree to end all hostilities so that amity may exist between those who have formerly been at war. Cowper says that peace always follows virtue and is its sure reward. The apostle Paul told the Ephesians that Christ "is our peace." (Ephesians 2:14.)

As Jesus was about to leave the earth, he promised

69

his followers: "Peace I leave with you, my peace I give unto you: not as the world giveth, give I unto you. Let not your heart be troubled, neither let it be afraid." (John 14:27.)

The most satisfying kind of peace is Christ's peace. That is a peace in which the cause of strife has been removed from us. Many people try to make their peace co-exist with their sins; however, it is pretty difficult to get peace by compact or negotiation or because of some dictated decree without having peace in ourselves. When some of the more influential European nations objected to Hitler's program for enslaving the weaker nations of Europe, he shouted back to them angrily, "Let us alone, we want peace." That is, he wanted peace while he enslaved the weaker nations without interference from anyone else. This is the kind of peace criminals want, the kind of peace that will enable them to carry out their own ungodly programs of crime unhampered by law and order.

All true peace must be based on righteousness. If we don't find peace within ourselves, we will not find it in any other place, and when sin and wrong get into our lives, peace disappears.

In one of the great prophecies for our day, the Lord looked forward to a time when peace would be taken from the earth and the devil would have power over his own dominion. In his own day, Jesus looked down to this condition in our time and foretold the conditions that would bring about the wars and other disturbances that would cover the earth as the direct result of evil.

While dreadful wars between nations are very destructive, they do not come close to equaling the destructiveness of the deadly private wars people frequently carry on between themselves. Moral diseases break down the mind, destroy balance in the nervous system, and damage the soul. The scriptures mention another kind of warfare when God said that the sins of the fathers would be visited upon the children, and Jesus said that a man's foes would be those of his own household. Isn't it interesting that we may pick up our worst sins from our best friends? Many children get their worst lessons in dishonesty, desertion, alcoholism, immorality, and other vices in their own homes from their own parents. Among the most prominent causes of spiritual failure, mental disease, nervous disorders, and personality problems are the hate and disease that come from broken homes. We should add to this total the deformities that take place in the millions of people who continue to live together under conditions of extreme strife, hate, and bickering.

Jesus indicated that peace would be taken from the earth because of the sins of the nations. Peace can also be taken from homes because of the crime, sin, failure, and weakness that is permitted to incarnate itself in the lives of one or both of the marrying partners. Neither love nor peace can long survive in the presence of immorality, irresponsibility, dishonesty, drunkenness, or laziness. When righteousness is taken out of the home, peace is automatically taken out of the hearts of those who live there.

Jesus said, "Contention is not of me." And yet contention, strife, name-calling, bickering, and severe unhappiness are part of the lives of many people who are forced to suffer the tortures of those partially and prematurely damned.

Recently I talked with a mother of seven children who had been divorced after many years of enduring these living torments. She had tried to establish in her children attitudes of righteousness, but her husband had been antagonistic and had made fun of her. He had used his rebellion against the church as an excuse for his violation of its laws. He had declared an unrighteous war against his wife and the church. It seemed to give him some kind of a satanic pleasure to hold a view as

71

opposite as possible from both of them. He has taken some joy in the fact that his children have largely identified with him instead of their mother, but they are now also becoming involved with him in all kinds of evil. In all of this, the mother has been the victim. Her peace has been taken from the earth, and there is no way that she can get it back so long as the evil of her family persists. How she would love to feel a little righteous pride in her family! She feels that she should be entitled to just a little happiness in her life before she dies. And it would seem like heaven to feel a little tranquillity in her heart, but as her problems go on increasing, her peace seems to become more and more impossible. Shakespeare seemed to have had her situation in mind when he said: "Each new morn new windows howl, new orphans cry, new sorrows strike heaven in the face."

When the Master said, "Blessed are the peacemakers: for they shall be called the children of God" (Matthew 5:9), he was not speaking merely to military leaders. I know a man who I think is a real peacemaker, and consequently he is very happy. He generates righteousness wherever he goes, and in his case, peace follows virtue as its sure reward. His primary concern as a husband is not to dominate his wife; his one ambition is to make her happy. He loves her wholeheartedly and does many nice little things that he knows will please her. His wife has absolute confidence and trust in him, and she has a comforting feeling of peace in her heart.

This man is also devoted to the Lord and is fully converted to the Lord's standards of righteousness. I think the Lord must trust him much as he did Job. He has a wonderful attitude and always does the right thing. He loves his children and teaches them righteousness. They are all happily associated together as a family. They all have confidence in their father and mother and in each other. They make up a happy family and are at peace.

I think of this man in contrast to those men mentioned about whom the Lord said: "For behold, I, the Lord, have seen the sorrow, and heard the mourning of the daughters of my people . . . because of the wickedness and abominations of their husbands. And I will not suffer, saith the Lord of Hosts, that the cries of the fair daughters of this people . . . shall come up against the men of my people, saith the Lord of Hosts. For they shall not lead away captive the daughters of my people because of their tenderness, save I shall visit them with a sore curse, even unto destruction; for they shall not commit whoredoms, like unto them of old, saith the Lord of Hosts." (Jacob 2:31-33.)

I am confident that the Lord was very upset when he spoke this condemnation. And I can picture that the men mentioned had taken a lot of peace from the earth as they had broken the hearts of their wives and lost the confidence of their children. Elbert Hubbard once said that in his opinion the unpardonable sin was incompatibility. When one understands the great amount of pain that the sins of one person may bring into the lives of many other people, the seriousness of the sin becomes even more evident. Bickering, quarreling, and hate can destroy the spirituality as well as the mental balance of people.

How wonderful are those referred to by Jesus when he said: "Blessed are the peacemakers: for they shall be called the children of God." When one stands before God, what could be more pleasing than to know that he has been an instrument of peace for his family, his employer, his friends, and God? May God help us all to be peacemakers.

A Dud

Much of Jesus's effective teaching ability came from his skillful use of parables. As he illustrated his ideas with appropriate stories he gave them greater life as well as power, color, and interest. Because he considered his ideas from every side, he strengthened his comparisons. Certainly the possibilities of his ideas were never exhausted by just one comparison.

Jesus used comparisons even when referring to himself. He said, "I am the light of the world." He compared himself to a door, to a shepherd, to a high tower. He said, "I am the way, the truth, and the light." He called himself "The good husbandman." He referred to himself as the "vinedresser."

Jesus made a rather unfavorable comparison for us when, as he looked beyond his own day down to our time, he said ". . . as the days of Noe were, so shall also the coming of the Son of man be." (Matthew 24:37.)

When Jesus referred to himself as the light of the world, as the wise teacher, or as the great physician, he was helping to lift himself up. However, frequently we go in the other direction and make our situations and ourselves worse off by a downgrading comparison. We emphasize our problems and our weaknesses, resulting in an inferiority complex. One of the most difficult burdens anyone has to bear is the feeling that his own life is not worthwhile.

Recently a young woman came to talk about her problems. She had discussed them with anyone who would listen, and each seemed to have made a different diagnosis and prescription. Each had touched a different problem, and in her mind this woman seemed to have accepted each criticism and turned it into a major sin. Problems are given us to overcome, not to pull us down or surrender ourselves to.

The other day I heard of a rather striking accusation of a man when someone referred to him as a dud. I was interested in this oppressive title—not because it was applied to this particular man, but because it may so often be applied to human nature generally. Certainly this is a trait that we should be on guard against. The man making the application was an engineer who works with explosives. Because I wanted to get a better picture of the human aspects of this trait, I looked up the meaning of the word *dud*.

The dictionary says that this term is usually applied to a bomb that fails to explode because of a defective fuse or some other small imperfection. Another more important meaning listed in the dictionary for the word *dud* and the situation that goes with it is one that applies more closely to human beings, for it refers to someone who is ineffective and unimpressive.

Someone has said that a man's failure can often be attributed to the fact that he uses blank cartridges when shooting at his targets. The meaning of *dud* might be expanded a little bit to include also those people whose firearms explode wrong or prematurely, sending their shrapnel in the wrong directions. A related term is *backfire*.

Every one of the parables of Jesus was intended to inspire improvement. Yet he frequently talked vigorously about negative ideas in order to increase the impact on the people for whom the shock was intended. Listen to some of his stinging comparisons to some members of the leading classes:

"Woe unto you, scribes and Pharisees, hypocrites! for ye are like unto whited sepulchres, which indeed appear beautiful outward, but are within full of dead men's bones, and of all uncleanness.

"Even so ye also outwardly appear righteous unto men, but within ye are full of hypocrisy and iniquity.

"Woe unto you, scribes and Pharisees, hypocrites!

75

because ye build the tombs of the prophets, and garnish the sepulchres of the righteous.

"And say, If we had been in the days of our fathers, we would not have been partakers with them in the blood of the prophets.

"Wherefore ye be witnesses unto yourselves, that ye are the children of them which killed the prophets." (Matthew 23:27-31.)

Again he said: "Woe unto you, scribes and Pharisees, hyprocrites! for ye make clean the outside of the cup and of the platter, but within they are full of extortion and excess." (Matthew 23:25.)

Jesus talked about the many evils that get into human beings, not with the idea of promoting those traits in them, but to help them overcome problems that might cause their deeds to backfire and destroy them.

The purpose of the Ten Commandments is to impress us with some of those things that we just must *not* do under any circumstances. To keep the commandments is the best way to prevent ourselves from becoming duds. God is all-wise, all-powerful, and all-good. If we live by his teachings, we can make ourselves effective instruments of his power.

When one develops defective ambitions or weak faith or questionable loyalty to God, he may wake up to find that he has made himself a dud. When a bomb fails, the engineer can usually get a new one, but what can anyone do who has a dud for a father or mother, a dud for a husband or wife, a dud for a son or daughter, or a dud for an employee?

All of God's teachings, the holy scriptures, the church, our parents, our brains, our conscience, and our ambition were designed to prevent us from being duds in every aspect of our lives. Every principle of the gospel was intended to help us to make the very best and the very most of our lives.

We can keep our power alive by charging ourselves

with the advice of Jesus, who said: "Ask, and it shall be given you; seek, and ye shall find; knock, and it shall be opened unto you." (Matthew 7:7.)

God is always anxious to help. He said: ". . . before they call, I will answer; and while they are yet speaking, I will hear." (Isaiah 65:24.)

The dictionary gives another definition for the word *dud*. Duds are ragged or cast-off clothing. Duds denote dirt and tatters and there are a lot of people today who dress in "duds." However, this is not the kind of clothing that God wears. When Jesus went up into the high mountain and, with Moses and Elias, was transfigured before Peter, James, and John, he appeared in shining garments "and his face did shine as the sun, and his raiment was white as the light." (Matthew 17:2.) May God help us to overcome unwise tendencies to be duds by developing the opposite quality of Godliness.

The Pursuit of Ugliness

Each of us has been endowed by the Creator with a number of inalienable rights that are ours as gifts from God. Some of these are the right to labor, the quest for excellence, the expectations of succeeding in our righteous efforts, the right to be judged according to our works, and the privilege of building up our own godliness. But sometimes things go wrong. Sometimes we so badly lose our bearings that we go in the wrong direction.

In a famous football game a few years ago, a player ran 95 yards in the wrong direction and scored a touchdown for his school's opponents. We may also remember back to 1938 when aviator Douglas Corrigan got into his airplane in New York, intending to go to Los Angeles, but instead he ended up in Dublin, Ireland. After that time he was referred to as "Wrong-way Corrigan."

Sometimes we distort the spirit of what we are doing. We get mixed up in our objectives. When we forget life's real purposes we may find ourselves in places where we don't want to be. The most notorious of all "Wrong-way Corrigans" was Lucifer. In the council in heaven he rebelled against God, and Isaiah says of him:

"How art thou fallen from heaven, O Lucifer, son of the morning! how art thou cut down to the ground, which didst weaken the nations!

"For thou hast said in thine heart, I will ascend into heaven, I will exalt my throne above the stars of God: I will sit also upon the mount of the congregation, in the sides of the north:

"I will ascend above the heights of the clouds; I will be like the most High.

"Yet thou shalt be brought down to hell, to the sides of the pit." (Isaiah 14:12-15.)

Lucifer started out to be like God, but because he traveled in the wrong direction, he became Satan and landed in hell.

One of our wrong-way excursions is our pursuit of ugliness. We have a brand of modern art that would have shocked the senses of the great artists of years past. Some of our music is coarse, loud, and degrading; it badly jars our senses when compared to those exquisite harmonies produced by the masters. In many cases even man, that great human masterpiece formed in God's own image and endowed with his possibilities, has defiled himself with several kinds of ugliness.

Some time ago Eugene Burdick and William Lederer wrote a book entitled *The Ugly American*. They pointed out some of the things about Americans that tend to give others a bad impression. Some early-day American settlers were confronted by tribes of savages who, in order to make a more terrifying impression on their foes, painted grotesque designs on their faces and, with the effects produced by war-paint and blood-curdling yells, sent chills of terror through their victims who were under attack.

Today we also have groups of people who seem to have turned away from beauty in favor of ugliness. They have ugliness in their dress, their speech, their thoughts, and their deeds. Any kind of evil immorality makes ugly scars in our faces and on our spirits. The puffy, bloated face, addled brain, and scrambled speech of an alcoholic could never be described as being beautiful. There are people who allow ugly tempers, hateful moods, and disgusting attitudes to load them up with the very ugliness of hell.

Recently a young man came to complain about the way he was being abused by society. He felt extremely sorry for himself. When he was a child, his grandfather had established a trust fund intended for his education under certain conditions. However, when he was eighteen, the trustees declined to turn over any part of the money to him on the grounds that he was not competent to use it, as his grandfather had instructed. They put him on probation for a couple of years and asked him to shape up. The two years have now passed and they contend that he is still not capable of handling the money.

When he was eighteen, he married a young woman a couple of months before their child was born. However, his wife refused to live with him and the court issued a restraining order, preventing him from seeing their child. This young man could have been a nice-looking person; he was also naturally intelligent. However, because of lack of grooming and the way he thinks and dresses, he has an extremely unattractive physical appearance. The selfishness of his mental

79

attitude has caused him some ugly public and social relationships, but he blames all of his problems on others.

I tried to assist him by helping him change his attitude. I suggested that many other people had gone to school who did not have wealthy grandfathers, and that he could easily prove his competence merely by being competent. I tried to suggest that he listen to the trustees and let them help him, but his hatred for them is too strong for him to overcome his faults.

Then I tried to sell him on the idea of what a great thrill it could be if he would change his attitude, get a haircut, take a bath, put on some clean, conventional clothing, and go to work.

But he kept repeating one of the usual plaints of some "wrong-way Corrigans" by saying, "I want people to like me for what I am—not for how I look." I suggested that he might easily solve that problem by looking, acting, thinking, and working like the man he wanted to be like. I suggested that we take a piece of paper and a pencil and make a list of those qualities that he "was" that he wanted people to like him for.

This young man had always taken it for granted that there was no need for him to do any improving. It didn't occur to him that he might have a distorted opinion of himself. Because he had never tried self-analysis, he knew of no place where he might improve. He wanted everyone to love him for what he assumed he was. He imagined that others should think of him as he thought of himself, which to him was completely satisfactory. But actually what was he? The record is clear that—

1. He was a drop-out from school.
2. He was unemployed and unemployable.
3. His heart was filled with bitterness and hate.
4. He was against almost all social conventions.
5. He didn't know how to have a reasonable discussion about himself.

6. He resented suggestions.

7. He was rebellious.

So far as I know, the best summary of his problems would be to say that he was ugly.

Many years ago Edwin Markham wrote a poem entitled *The Man with the Hoe*. He gives us a depressing picture of one kind of a life as he says:

Bowed by the weight of centuries he leans
Upon his hoe and gazes on the ground,
The emptiness of ages in his face,
And on his back the burden of the world.

Who made him dumb to rapture and despair,
A thing that grieves not and that never hopes,
Stolid and stunned, brother to the ox?
Who loosened and let down this brutal jaw,
Whose was the hand that slanted back this brow?
Whose breath blew out the light within this brain?

Is this the Thing the Lord God made and gave
To have dominion over sea and land,
To trace the stars and search the heavens for power,
And feel the passion of Eternity?
Is this the Dream He dreamed who shaped the suns
And pillared the blue firmament with light?
Down all the stretch of hell to its last gulf
There is no shape more terrible than this.

While this is an awful picture of life, yet it is nonviolent and will cause only pity in the hearts of people. It is much more terrible when a human being makes a commitment to a contagious ugliness, in which both he himself and others are going to be the losers.

God can resurrect a dead body, and he can also put a light back in a defective brain. But what can he do for one who loves evil and ugliness? God has said, ". . . he which is filthy, let him be filthy still." (Revelation 22:11.) God has provided that in the world to come we will associate with those of our own kind. Those who get themselves most deeply involved in sin will be compelled to live with it forever as companions of the devil and his angels, who have made evil their specialty.

Suppose each one of us were to check up on ourselves and make up a list of those traits of ugliness, large or small, that are being permitted to grow in our lives. There is a characteristic of ugliness in uncleanness. There is ugliness in disorder, in failure, and in disobedience to God. There is ugliness in unfairness and in hate, anger, and revenge. After we have done a little checking up we may discover that we need to have a good housecleaning and then reverse our philosophy and make some good, strong commitments to beauty, order, and righteousness.

We may all have as much as we like of the beauty of cleanliness and the beauty of accomplishment. We can have beauty in our attitudes and beauty in our ideals. Emerson said that "beauty is the mark which God sets on virtue." When we are properly virtuous, God puts a light in our eyes and a spring in our step and a radiance in our hearts. It is our virtues that entitle us to a glorious resurrection where we can live forever in the presence of God.

Courtesy

Some time ago, a young woman asked if I would prepare some kind of a discussion on courtesy. I asked her why she was making this request. She, with some friends, had attended an athletic event and had been sitting by some disorderly people who were very rude in their behavior. They had been ill-mannered and disrespectful toward an older man seated nearby. She had been so disturbed that she wanted someone to write about it and to put some thoughts together in such a way that it might help reduce future offenses of such discourtesy.

Although this young woman had not been the direct victim of the discourtesy, she had been hurt with a kind of pain that had tended to make her physically and spiritually ill. I told her I thought she should be the one to write down ideas about courtesy while they had such a forceful hold on her emotions. I do not know whether she will do this or not. I hope she does, because her feelings were so strong about it and might be productive of good not only for herself but also for others. However, as I thought about it a little more, I decided that this is something that I myself should also do, for when we write something down, we are encouraged to give it more consideration and to think about it more effectively in our minds. This in turn helps us build up the individual quality of our lives.

The dictionary says that courtesy is well-mannered conduct and indicates a respect for or a consideration of other people. E. M. Forster says that "courtesy is the civil deed that shows the good heart." A courteous person is one who is fine-souled, who has a genuine desire to do good, to help others and make them happy.

M. A. Kelty said, "Small kindnesses, small courtesies, small considerations, habitually practiced in our social intercourse, give a greater charm to the character than the display of great talents or great accomplishments." Goethe declared, "There is no outward sign of true courtesy that does not rest on a deep moral foundation." And Emerson said, "We should be as courteous to a man as we are to a picture, which we are willing to give the advantage of the best possible light."

People do many fine things for others because of courtesy. Such people don't expect pay or other return considerations. They do it because they are that kind of people and their actions identify them as gracious, kindly, helpful, and loving human beings who are trying to lift people up and make the world better.

Many young people are discourteous to those who are old or infirm or do not have the strength and abilities that they themselves possess. One group of boys put a rattlesnake in a box and then with sticks poked and hit and tortured it to see it strike and hear it hiss and rattle. They finally made the rattlesnake so angry that it bit itself to death. We sometimes do about that same thing to people.

Almost everywhere we go we see the results of vandalism, crime, and sin that come out of the kind of nature that starts out merely by being discourteous. One group of boys burned down a schoolhouse; another group destroyed the plaques on some historic pioneer memorials. People sometimes spread false rumors, say unkind things, and indulge in other forms of discourtesy. One who is profane is discourteous to God, and everyone who sets a bad example or causes problems for others is discourteous to those around him.

I know a man who at one time was a heavy user of cigarettes, which he decided to quit. Now when he is in a room with smokers where he is compelled to breathe the cigarette fumes, his face bloats up and afterwards he is physically ill. It is well known to all smokers that there are many people to whom cigarette smoke is offensive; yet many of them blow their smoke around with a complete disregard for the most simple rules of courtesy.

Many of the things we do that offend others come about because of thoughtlessness on our part. Recently I attended a church meeting for which a fine program had been prepared. There were several hundred people in attendance. Three young women with crying babies sat all through the meeting and thoughtlessly permitted their children to disturb those in attendance.

Shakespeare's Portia said of mercy: "It blesseth him that gives and him that takes." The same thing could properly be said of courtesy. It is pleasant to the one who receives it and it has a constructive, refining influence on the one who practices it. A mother will build many desirable traits in herself as well as in her children by teaching them from the very earliest age to always be reverent and courteous in their attitudes.

It is reported that Joan of Arc would allow no crude conduct in her soldiers; on one occasion she said: "Even the rude business of war can better be conducted without profanity and the other brutalities of speech." We learn to do by doing, and the more we practice discourtesy, the more that offensive quality gets into us.

One of the wisest decisions we can make is to always be courteous, kind, and gracious. A courteous person does not violate the rules of accepted conduct. A courteous person is not immodest or offensive. He is always thoughtful of God, of his country, of his family, of his friends, and even of his enemies.

May we always be courteous in our speech, in our activities, in our appearance. Then, when we go to stand before God, it is likely that one of the qualities that will shine brighter in our lives than almost any other is that great gem of courtesy.

Good
Judgment

No matter how many other virtues we may have, if we don't have good judgment, then, as the apostle Paul says, we "become as sounding brass, or a tinkling cymbal." (1 Corinthians 13:1.)

With good, solid, dependable, discriminating judgment, we may have good things not only in this life but also in the next. When we think of judgments given in courts of law, we often turn for inspiration to Areopagus, that most celebrated ancient court which held its sessions in Athens on Mar's Hill, west of the Acropolis. This is where the apostle Paul went to expound the principles of his religion. This court was made up of the wisest, most highly respected men available. All parties to a dispute were required to present the truth so the judges could give proper decisions. The judges built up such a fine reputation for wisdom that people came from many other nations to have their problems solved.

Good judgment increases the value of every other virtue and ability. It is an interesting idea that no one can go through a single day without holding his own court many times. Whether one is a housewife, a child, or the head of a great business organization, every day brings many new things that must be considered, evaluated, and decided upon. Only one who has good judgment can maintain proper order in his life and create advantages out of that vast jungle of good and bad alternatives that everyone is confronted with.

The opposite of wisdom is foolishness. Since time began, the harsh term *fool* has been used to describe one who has poor judgment. An old axiom says that "the fool and his money are soon parted." The scripture says: "The fool hath said in his heart, there is no God." (Psalm 14:1.) One can easily make himself a fool merely by doing foolish things, and when he fully understands this process, then he already has a part of the formula as to how to become wise.

Someone once said to his friend that he would give anything to know where he was going to die. His friend said, "What good would that do you?" He replied, "If I knew where I was going to die, then I would never go around the place." When we know what makes one a fool, then we can cut off all indulgence in that area.

A criminal is a fool. A sinner is a fool. An idler is a fool. One who gives way to his temper is a fool. One who thinks with his prejudices or his sex urges or his hates is a fool. These are all things that we should stay away from.

Because King Saul disobeyed God, he was rejected from being king. About this event, Saul said, "I have sinned: . . . I have played the fool and have erred exceedingly." (1 Samuel 26:21.) In the Bible concordance there are about as many references to fools as to sinners. To the man who tore down his barns to build them larger, God said, "Thou fool, this night thy soul shall be required of thee." (Luke 12:20.) He didn't say that the man was a sinner; he just didn't have good judgment. Many passages in the scriptures can help us identify our own foolishness so that we can then keep away from it. Solomon, the wise man, said:

"The way of a fool is right in his own eyes: but he that hearkeneth unto counsel is wise." (Proverbs 12:15.)

"A fool despiseth his father's instruction: but he that regardeth reproof is prudent." (Proverbs 15:5.)

"A fool hath no delight in understanding. . . ." (Proverbs 18:2.)

"Answer not a fool according to his folly, lest thou also be like unto him." (Proverbs 26:4.)

"And the king [David] lamented over Abner, and said, Died Abner as a fool dieth?" (2 Samuel 3:33.)

"The fear of the Lord is the beginning of knowledge: but fools despise wisdom and instruction." (Proverbs 1:7.)

A single bad choice may cause one an entire lifetime of suffering. We can learn to make better judgments by studying models of excellence and making firm, long-term decisions based on God's standards of right and wrong. We can also increase the quality of our judgment by learning to understand what causes weakness and foolishness. Then, by contrast and elimination, we can more effectively learn the companion art of discrimination in building up our own judgment.

With a well-trained conscience and a set of good habits, we can learn to increase our judgment. Too many faults and too many weaknesses can make fools out of even wise men, whereas the integrity and strength of high personal codes of honor will put inferior procedures out of bounds where they are not eligible for consideration.

People's lives turn on very small hinges, and some of the smallest decisions may seem of little consequence when they are made. Yet even small decisions can make us both fools and failures.

Sound judgment helps us to see things in the light of their consequences. Good judgment is the highest crown that can be placed on human intelligence, enabling one to choose what is proper as against that which is improper. Of the multiplicity of paths that may be taken in our lives, there is always one path that is better than the others, and it is our responsibility to find it and walk in it. We transgress the laws of right only because we make faulty choices between alternatives. It is so common to choose the easier rather than the better path, or to take the popular course instead of the right one.

We need to learn to see causes and effects in their true relationship. A person who makes decisions without relation to their consequences will live in a constant state of chaos in his emotions and confusion in his judgment. Sound decisions are not always easy in the heat of chaos in our minds unless we have done our homework in periods of quiet thoughtfulness.

A substitute football quarterback, sitting on the bench during a game, may improve his own judgment and skill by practicing his plays as the game proceeds even though he is not in it. While others are making the real decisions on the field, he can be making them on the bench; then he is able to check his judgment against others in the light of what happens. We can also learn to check up on ourselves and to distinguish between superior and inferior philosophies by comparing them with those that have been proved by time.

God was trying to train us in good judgment when he said: "Come now, and let us reason together," (Isaiah 1:18.) He said: "Learn to do well; seek judgment, relieve the oppressed, judge the fatherless, plead for the widow." (Isaiah 1:17.)

We know about those many things which God says are wrong. We also know the many things he says are right. We can learn to reason by comparing our own reason with God's judgment, and one of the best ways to become as God is, is to learn to think and reason as he does.

The Ways of Pleasantness

One concern every human being should have is to know the kind of person he is making of himself. Each person has many choices as to what he may become. He may become a rich man, a poor man, a beggarman, a thief, a doctor, a lawyer, a merchant, a chief. Regardless of what one becomes, though, he ought to try always to be friendly, kind, and pleasant. The ability to make others happy adds greatly to any other ability we may develop. A good man who is pleasant is much better than a good man who is unpleasant.

One of the greatest compliments ever given to anyone was given by God the Father to his most capable and righteous Son when, on four different occasions, he introduced his Only Begotten in the flesh by saying,

89

"This is my Beloved Son, in whom I am well pleased." And one of the greatest compliments that we could receive would be to have our friends, our associates, and our family members say that we are the kind of person in whom they are well pleased.

Recently a letter giving the opposite of this situation appeared in a "trouble" column of a newspaper. It said:

"We have three grown children, all raised in a good Christian home with good examples to follow. But there's not one we can brag about.

"They're all college graduates, but they might just as well have been high school dropouts for all the good their education has done them.

"The oldest, a son, 30, plays guitar with a rock group. He dresses like a bum, his eyes are always bloodshot, he's a vegetarian, skinny as a beanpole, and he's always dead tired. He has no plans for the future, and the only good thing we can say for him is he never asks us for money.

"The two girls are another story. The 27-year-old lives in Mexico with a married man. She says he's an artist. She's supposed to be teaching English to Mexicans, but she always needs money. We send her half of what she asks for because I can't sleep thinking she may be hungry.

"The 24-year-old is living with a group of people who are into some far-out religious cult. They meditate a lot, don't believe in working to provide for themselves, but she's always asking for donations to feed herself and her brothers and sisters who seem to have her hypnotized.

"Where did we go wrong? And what do we tell people who ask about our children? [Signed] Embarrassed."

What an unwise and unprofitable way to spend one's life—causing embarrassment to those people who should have great love and enthusiasm for us. And what a thrilling idea it is to think that any one of us with the right kind of attitudes and behavior could actually please everyone, including God himself, and give all a great thrill of happy sensations and exhilarating feelings!

Anyone who is so inclined may be a friendly neighbor, a friendly husband, or a friendly employee. There may be some good people whom we respect and whom we admire but who make us feel uncomfortable and unhappy while we are around them.

In the scriptures Solomon makes many important arguments in favor of developing wisdom; he paid wisdom its greatest compliment when he said: "Her ways are ways of pleasantness, and all her paths are peace. She is a tree of life to them that lay hold upon her: and happy is every one that retaineth her. The Lord by wisdom hath founded the earth; by understanding hath he established the heavens." (Proverbs 3:17-19.)

When we add pleasantness to our wisdom and understanding, we find the shortest way to many successes. As Shakespeare said, "No profit grows where is no pleasure ta'en." Those things that are most profitable are those which we have the greatest joy in doing. That which we do well is pleasant, and that which we do not do well is unpleasant.

For far too many people traveling the roadway of life, the atmosphere is filled with bitterness and the unpleasantness of arguments, bickering, unfriendliness, and disagreeableness. The biggest problem of many is that they just can't get along with others. Each of us might well check up on our activities as they relate to those with whom we travel along life's highway and see what we can do to make their journey with us more pleasureable and joyful. Or we might make an inventory of our own unpleasantness, determine what can be done about it, and find ways to be more agreeable and bring more joy to those with whom we associate.

It is a fine art to know how to live well. Benjamin

91

Franklin once wrote a parable that he entitled "Brotherly Love." In order to treat such a lofty theme, he fittingly adopted a biblical style and language. It is said that he used to take great delight in reading this parable to his friends, who were often puzzled when asked to tell in what part of the Bible it was found.

A Parable on Brotherly Love

1. In those days there was no worker of iron in all the land. And the merchants of Midian passed by with their camels, bearing spices, and myrrh, and balm, and wares of iron.

2. And Reuben bought an ax of the Ismaelite merchants which he prized highly, for there was none in his father's house.

3. And Simeon said to Reuben, his brother, "Lend me, I pray thee, thine ax." But he refused, and would not.

4. And Levi also said unto him, "My brother, lend me, I pray thee, thine ax." And he refused him also.

5. Then came Judah unto Reuben, and entreated him, saying, "Lo, thou lovest me, and I have always loved thee; do not refuse me the use of thine ax."

6. But Reuben turned from him, and refused him likewise.

7. Now it came to pass that Reuben hewed timber on the bank of the river, and his ax fell therein, and he could by no means find it.

8. But Simeon, Levi, and Judah had sent a messenger after the Ismaelites, with money, and had bought for themselves each an ax.

9. Then came Reuben unto Simeon, and said, "Lo, I have lost mine ax, and my work is unfinished: lend me thine, I pray thee."

10. And Simeon answered him, saying, "Thou wouldst not lend me thine ax; therefore will I not lend thee mine."

11. Then went he unto Levi, and said unto him, "My brother, thou knowest my loss and my necessity; lend me, I pray thee, thine ax."

12. And Levi reproached him, saying, "Thou wouldst not lend me thine ax when I desired it; but I will be better than thou, and will I lend thee mine."

13. And Reuben was grieved at the rebuke of Levi, and, being ashamed, turned from him, and took not the ax, but sought his brother Judah.

14. And as he drew near, Judah beheld his countenance as it were covered with grief and shame; and he prevented him, saying, "My brother, I know thy loss, but why should it trouble thee? Lo, have I not an ax that will serve both thee and me? Take it, I pray thee, and use it as thine own."

15. And Reuben fell upon his neck, and kissed him with tears, saying, "Thy kindness is great, but thy goodness in forgiving me is greater. Thou art indeed my brother, and whilst I live will I surely love thee."

16. And Judah said, "Let us also love our other brethren; behold, are we not all of one blood?"

17. And Joseph saw these things, and reported them to his father, Jacob.

18. And Jacob said, "Reuben did wrong, but he repented; Simeon also did wrong; and Levi was not altogether blameless. But the heart of Judah is princely. Judah has the soul of a king. His father's children shall bow down before him, and he shall rule over his brethren."

In Mr. Franklin's parable, Judah may not have been more intelligent, more courageous, or more industrious than his other brothers, but he became the leader because he was more kind, more wise, and more pleasant. He did not want to cause embarrassment or bring acknowledgment or credit to himself. Jacob might well have said of Judah, "This is my beloved son, in whom I am well pleased."

What a great opportunity life offers us to be pleasant to our husbands or wives, our families, our employers, our employees, our God.

Lest
We Forget

One of the great national rulers of our world was Queen Victoria of Great Britain. A crown was placed upon her head when she was in her teens. During her long reign, ending at her death in 1901, England became the greatest nation that had ever existed upon the earth. Victoria ruled a territory that included over 25 percent of all of the earth's surface. Her navies ruled the seven seas, and the sun never set on the British Empire.

One of the important events occurring during her rule was her Diamond Jubilee, marking the sixtieth year of her notable reign. In commemoration of the jubilee, the London *Times* asked Rudyard Kipling to write an appropriate poem. The result was his famous "Recessional." The dictionary says that a recessional is something that marks a retreat, a song played while the audience is leaving, a hymn sung as the clergy and the choir are retiring from the chancel to the robing room. Rudyard Kipling had some ideas about another kind of recessional.

In order to appreciate this poem, we might try to picture the pomp and pageantry of this jubilee of 1897 when England was at the height of her power. To this magnificent celebration came princes from the Far East and ambassadors from the royal houses of Europe. There were vast military and naval displays, and a tremendous civic celebration with processions and public services, all united to pour out a nation's adulation and praise to England's queen.

To Mr. Kipling, the empire, in its dream of pride and power, had seemed to lose sight of the King of kings, and as the armies returned to their posts, the navies departed for their far-away island possessions, the kings and chiefs returned home, and the jubilation died away, he pointed out their similarity to some of the other great nations of the past. His recessional was intended to recall the nation from its dream of pride and power. Within a few months after its publication, this poem became one of the most widely known and admired in the language.

On one occasion Victoria was asked why England had so far excelled all other nations of the earth. She laid her hand upon the Bible and said, "England is the land of the book," and for a long time so it was. As long as England lived by the precepts of the scriptures, her greatness continued to accelerate. But just as celebrations sometimes come to an end, so greatness and faith can also go into a recession or a retreat. And seventy-six years after Victoria's jubilee, Rudyard Kipling might still be saying to us:

God of our fathers, known of old—
  Lord of our far-flung battle line—
Beneath Whose awful hand we hold
  Dominion over palm and pine—
Lord God of Hosts, be with us yet,
  Lest we forget—lest we forget!

The tumult and the shouting dies;
  The captains and the kings depart:
Still stands Thine ancient Sacrifice,
  An humble and a contrite heart.
Lord God of Hosts, be with us yet,
  Lest we forget—lest we forget!

Far-called, our navies melt away;
  On dune and headland sinks the fire:
Lo, all our pomp of yesterday
  Is one with Nineveh and Tyre!
Judge of the Nations, spare us yet,
  Lest we forget—lest we forget!

If, drunk, with sight of power, we loose
Wild tongues that have not Thee in awe—
Such boasting as the Gentiles use
Or lesser breeds without the Law—
Lord God of Hosts, be with us yet,
Lest we forget—lest we forget!

For heathen heart that puts her trust
In reeking tube and iron shard—
All valiant dust that builds on dust,
And guarding, calls not Thee to guard—
For frantic boast and foolish word,
Thy mercy on Thy people, Lord!
Amen.

Rudyard Kipling's poem still has great religious as well as human significance. It recalls when similar ambitions may have been celebrated in the ancient kingdoms of Nineveh and Tyre, which had forgotten the contents of their own speeches and proclamations made in the days when they had celebrated their greatness with festivities and military fanfare. Many of us also become drunk with our own importance and the possibilities of our own power, and we loose wild tongues that belie the rulership of God and the purpose of our own lives.

We are reminded that some thirty-five centuries before Victoria, the Lord God of Hosts himself gathered the children of Israel together at the foot of Mount Sinai to make a covenant with them which, if they would keep it, would make them the greatest nation upon the earth. God came down onto the mount in a cloud of fire with such great power that the mountains shook and the people trembled. Then, to the accompaniment of lightnings and thunders, he gave that set of laws by which true greatness could be won and maintained.

But after the commandments had been given, God

also returned to his station. The fires died out on the mount. The lightning and thunders ceased. In Mr. Kipling's words, "the tumult and the shouting" died, and the people were dispersed to continue their journey toward their promised land. And when the excitement was past, this was exactly the time for the people to begin taking action.

Among other things, the Lord wanted the people to remember to do all the things he had talked to them about. But unfortunately they forgot many of these things. When the tumult and the shouting was over, many of them went back to their golden calves and their other sins. If they had kept running through their minds Mr. Kipling's refrain—"Lord God of Hosts, be with us yet, lest we forget—lest we forget"—they would not have been kept wandering in the wilderness for forty years until all of the original company but two had been denied their objectives and had perished in the wilderness.

Someday the festivities of our lives themselves will also come to an end. Our activities will be over, and the fires of our lives will have died down. Then the real work of life will be about ready to begin. Death is the key that unlocks the mansions of eternity. Then will be the time for blessings that we sang about to be realized. In the meantime, may God help us to live by the book so that we may begin our immortal lives with no depressions or recessionals, and so we may pray with Mr. Kipling, "Lord God of Hosts, be with us yet, Lest we forget—lest we forget!"

3

USING WISDOM
IN OUR ACTIONS

"And keep the charge of the Lord thy God,
to walk in his way, to keep his statutes,
and his commandments, and
his judgments, and his testimonies, . . .
that thou mayest prosper in all
that thou doest, and whithersoever
thou turnest thyself."

Wisdom Is
Where You Find It

Every person who desires to be successful in life should be able to bring to his work as many as possible of the ideas, inventions, and skills that have already been perfected by others. Many people have developed great expertise in their own lives, and their skills may well be appropriated by us for our own accomplishment.

Knute Rockne got his idea for glamorizing the uniforms of his football team by watching the chorus line at a theater. Orville and Wilbur Wright studied bees and birds to get ideas for their airplane. A smallpox serum was invented by a doctor studying a milkmaid who had cowpox. Penicillin was developed from mold.

Jesus had something like this in mind when he told the story of the steward of the rich man. He also indicated that worldly people are sometimes wiser than those who are known as the children of light. I understand this to mean that sometimes persons involved in a particular activity may close their minds and cease learning from others who are better students of what is happening in the world around them. I think the Lord intended that those to whom he referred as the children of light should keep their eyes open for all usable truths, from whatever source. He gave a helpful suggestion when he said, "Make to yourselves friends of the mammon of unrighteousness." (Luke 16:9.) I don't think he meant that one should adopt unrighteous ideas, but there are a lot of useful ideas developed by others that can be used by the children of light.

Jesus gave us another helpful idea for our own development when he declared: "He that is faithful in that which is least is faithful also in much: and he that is unjust in the least is unjust also in much.

"If therefore ye have not been faithful in the

unrighteous mammon, who will commit to your trust the true riches?

"And if ye have not been faithful in that which is another man's, who shall give you that which is your own?" (Luke 16:10-12.)

If we do not develop wisdom in our own affairs, our own thinking, and our own families, certainly it will not be available when a crisis comes along. And if we cannot be profitable to ourselves, how can we expect the Lord or anyone else to trust us with their affairs?

In carrying on the work of the world, we actually develop many of the skills that will enable us to be more effective in carrying on the work of the Lord, and vice versa. At their best, the work of the world and the work of the Lord can be closely related, for the Lord has said that to him all things are spiritual. Our skills should be directed toward success and should be capable of being profitable in any place when they are properly employed. It has been said that an institution is but the lengthened shadow of the men who built it. Should our efforts be involved in building temples or in building skyscrapers, those who invest in what we do will be most interested in finding out what kind of people we are. They will also want to know where we are going and how far. If one is wise enough to be responsible, everyone will be better off as a consequence.

When Andrew Carnegie was once asked to speak to the members of a college graduating class, he said, "I desire to speak only to those who want to be millionaires." He meant that he was interested only in speaking to those who had the industry, the courage, and the ambition to amount to something. Ordinarily no one invests his money with the idea of going broke, and no wise person cultivates relationships with those who are irresponsible. If we are to succeed, our abilities should be the kinds that are negotiable in any environment, against any kind of competition.

To qualify for the title of children of light, we ought to be wiser, better informed, more dependable, and more profitable in our associations than any other people. Wisdom will make us rich toward God. It will make us rich in our associations with other people. It will make us rich in our material affairs.

Some may ask, "Where can wisdom be found? How do we go about getting full possession of it?" There are many answers. Ralph Waldo Emerson said that we live in the lap of an immense intelligence, and wisdom is all around us. It is found on the printed page, on television and radio, and on film. It is in our sermons and our prayers.

Creation itself has given us a miraculous aid to wisdom: a conscience. When our first parents ate the fruit from the tree of knowledge of good and evil, God said, ". . . the man is [now] become as one of us to know good and evil. . . ." (Moses 4:28.) We also have available the wisdom of God, the wisdom of the prophets, the wisdom of great men and women. If we are to be wise, we must think wisely and act wisely.

It is not difficult to distinguish between wisdom and foolishness when these traits are displayed in someone else. The difficult thing is to learn to recognize these conditions in ourselves. An old axiom says that a man is judged by the company he keeps, and wisdom and good judgment keep the finest company.

The apostle Paul said something about charity that applies equally to wisdom. He might have said, "Wisdom doth not behave itself unseemly, seeketh not her own, is not easily provoked, thinketh no evil; rejoiceth not in iniquity, but rejoiceth in the truth." (See 1 Corinthians 13:5.) We might add, "If there is anything lovely, virtuous, praiseworthy, of good report, or *filled with wisdom*, we seek after these things." (See Article of Faith 13.)

People Changers

The most important assets of our universe are people, and the most important events that ever take place upon our planet are those events which improve human nature and human fortunes. We live in a world of opposites, and it seems that our ability to progress is usually about equal to our ability to retrogress. The main fact of our universe is the conflict of these two powerful forces, one attempting to lift us up and the other exerting all of its influence to drag us down.

If we could make a chart of our world's progress, it might resemble a graph showing the ups and downs of an erratic stock market. The depression periods would show extreme low levels in the days of Noah and Sodom and Gomorrah. Babylon is still noted for its wickedness, and the ancient empire of Rome reached an all-time level.

Most people making the graph for our own day would show some high peaks of scientific accomplishment, knowledge explosions, and business prosperity, but would probably picture a steadily descending line indicating a worsening of morality, a weakening in righteousness, a declining interest in the scriptures, a lessening in patriotism, and an upsurge in degeneracy.

The natural settling process that goes on in our society where we tend to come to rest at some low level makes the idea of lifting people up of the greatest possible importance. And yet so many of us turn off our engines, so to speak, and drift downward to one of the lower levels of life.

God has made a firm commitment to free agency, but he has placed a great many influences in the world to change us upward. President David O. McKay once said that the purpose of the gospel is to change people, to make bad men good and good men better. However, there are many people who want to change their circumstances, but who are unwilling to change themselves.

There are many institutions and influences in life designed to change people. Governments were instituted by God for the benefit of man, and God will hold us responsible for our acts in relationship to the government in making good laws and seeing that they are enforced.

Our occupations lift us up by teaching us the skills and attitudes of successfully making a living. Our entire culture is organized to make us honest, dependable, law-abiding citizens.

We have another set of powerful people changers in the great books that are so easily available to us. The famous educator Horace Mann once said, "A house without books is like a room without windows." No man has the right to bring up his children without surrounding them with good books. Children learn to read by being in the presence of good reading material. The love of knowledge comes from reading and grows upon us, and the love of knowledge in the young mind is almost a warrant against the inferior excitement of passion and vices. Of course, the greatest of our great books are the holy scriptures, in which we may make available to ourselves the direct word of the Lord as well as the prophets whom he has inspired.

Daniel Webster said, "If religious books are not widely circulated among the masses in this country and if the people do not become religious, I do not know what is to become of us as a nation. And the thought is one to cause solemn reflection on the part of every patriot and every Christian. If truth is not diffused, error will be. If God and his word are not known and received, the devil and his works will gain the ascendancy. If the evangelical volume does not reach

103

every hamlet, the pages of a corrupt and licentious literature will. If the power of the gospel is not felt through the length and breadth of the land, anarchy and misrule, degradation and misery, corruption and darkness will reign."

Another important influence for our benefit is found in trusty, well-selected, close friends. The greatest power in the world is the power of example. We tend to think and do those things which we see and hear other people do and say. The phrase "everybody's doing it" usually has a downhill connotation, but those great deeds done by our heroes can quickly change our lives into something much more worthwhile.

But the greatest of all people changers is ourselves. Whether we like it or not, we are being modified every day, and every hour we are becoming something that we have never before been. The scriptures speak of laying off the old man of sin and taking on the new man of righteousness. If we continue to keep ourselves under the right influences, we can soon be new persons embodying all of the right qualities. One of our problems is that we are not always consistent. Instead of going continually toward the goal, we go up and down, backward and forward, alternating between good and bad, failure and success.

The whole human family is supposed to be on a continual uphill march. However, when we do ten good things and then make ten exceptions, we are doing as much toward tearing down as we are toward building up.

After the Lord had healed the impotent man, he gave him this significant counsel: ". . . sin no more, lest a worst thing come unto thee." (John 5:14.) This indicates a significant possibility for all of us. The apostle Peter pointed out the serious nature of a mere temporary righteousness when he said:

"For if after they have escaped the pollutions of the

world through the knowledge of the Lord and Saviour Jesus Christ, they are again entangled therein, and overcome, the latter end is worse with them than the beginning.

"For it had been better for them not to have known the way of righteousness, than, after they have known it, to turn from the holy commandments delivered unto them.

"But it is happened unto them according to the true proverb, The dog is turned to his own vomit again; and the sow that was washed to her wallowing in the mire." (2 Peter 2:20-22.)

Permanent upward changes are the valuable kind. Francis Bacon once said:

It is not what we eat,
But what we digest, that makes us strong.
It is not what we read,
But what we remember, that makes us wise.
It is not what we think,
But what we do, that makes us successful.
It is not what we earn,
But what we save, that makes us rich.
It is not what we preach,
But what we practice, that makes us Christians.

And so we return again to this great idea that the most important responsibility in the world is that of changing people upward on a permanent basis. Everything that makes people more miserable, more unhappy, or more unfaithful is bad, and everything that makes people more faithful, more industrious, more beautiful, and more holy is good.

Where Much
Is Given

One of our greatest sources of interest in life is centered in our standard of living. We have a natural human tendency to like fine things. We enjoy nice homes, good food, and pleasant people with whom to associate. We also are the beneficiaries of the greatest knowledge explosion that has ever been known. We have the greatest educational opportunities and the highest standard of living ever before in history. In addition, we have the judgment of time shining upon the life of Christ. We have volumes of scripture with an authoritative "thus saith the Lord" attached to every doctrine. Our modern printing developments give us an intimate command of the greatest literature and enable us to share the most provocative experiences of all past ages. We know which activities of individuals and nations have brought both reward and destruction. The gospel of Jesus Christ has again been restored, and, as of old, prophets of the Lord again walk the earth.

The scriptures say that no man lives unto himself alone. Nothing could be further from the truth than to say to ourselves, "What I do is my own business." What we do is also God's business. He has commanded us to repent and be baptized. He has asked that we join his church and conduct ourselves according to his doctrines. We have an obligation and an opportunity to make him a party to our eternal marriages and govern our families according to his laws. We ourselves belong to him.

The apostle Paul said: "What? know ye not that your body is the temple of the Holy Ghost which is in you, which ye have of God, and ye are not your own? For ye are bought with a price: therefore glorify God in your body, and in your spirit, which are God's." (1 Corinthians 6:19-20.)

The scripture says: ". . . the Spirit [of God] enlighteneth every man through the world, that hearkeneth to the voice of the Spirit." (D&C 84:46.) We belong to him. We are dependent upon him. In a modern-day scripture the Lord has given us one of the important laws of consequence when he said, "For of him unto whom much is given much is required. . . ." (D&C 82:3.)

When we come into this world as human beings, we bring with us instinctive knowledge and the ability to learn. We brought much of it with us from God. William Wordsworth once wrote a philosophy in which he said:

Our birth is but a sleep and a forgetting;
The Soul that rises with us, our life's Star,
Hath had elsewhere its setting
And cometh from afar;
Not in entire forgetfulness,
And not in utter nakedness,
But trailing clouds of glory do we come
From God, who is our home.
("Ode on Intimations of Immortality")

And while, for a good purpose, our memory of our antemortal lives has been temporarily withheld from us, yet for a long pre-earth period we lived with God, where we became what we are and where in our natural growth we learned many things. And unless we deliberately distort our own intelligence, turn off our reason, and smother the whispering of the Spirit, we cannot help but know right from wrong and good from evil. We are intelligent people.

Some people may claim that there is no harm in stealing from the government or from some wealthy corporation. But that is only because they let evil overrule their judgment or intelligence. Everyone knows that to take property that belongs to someone else is wrong. We have many divine instincts, such as those

107

governing our self-preservation and our reproduction instincts. We have instincts for fairness and right. With a few minutes of thought anyone could figure out that those who keep the Sabbath day holy will, over their lifetimes, be different people from those who do not keep the Sabbath day holy. And when God has given us this power to reason, we are obligated to use it.

We can all know that we ought to honor our parents and that we ought to obey God rather than man. No one has a right to do wrong. We are not free to conduct ourselves as we please. What we do is the business of every other person in the world. We distort our own intelligence and deceive ourselves when we sin against our own conscience. Many of our most serious sins are not written in the statute books. For example, just think what great errors we make when we sin against reason, against intuition, and against instinct. And one of our greatest sins is when we sin against knowledge.

When Adam and Eve partook of the fruit of the tree of knowledge of good and evil, they were given a natural instinctive ability to know right from wrong. Then God said: "Behold, the man is now become as one of us to know good and evil." (Moses 4:28.)

Those who commit the greatest sins are called sons of perdition or sons of Satan. They are the ones who sin against the greatest knowledge. But to sin against any knowledge is serious. We have the responsibility to use every one of the abilities as well as the possibilities that God has given us. These great gifts obligate us to study, to learn, to think, and to reason, and when we do this, then the Lord gives us more. Paul said to the Hebrews:

"For it is impossible for those who were once enlightened, and have tasted of the heavenly gift, and were made partakers of the Holy Ghost,

"And have tasted the good word of God, and the powers of the world to come,

"If they shall fall away, to renew them again unto

repentance; seeing they crucify to themselves the Son of God afresh, and put him to an open shame." (Hebrews 6:4-8.)

The Lord has given us the power of repentance, which also carries some corresponding obligations. The apostle Peter said:

"For if after they have escaped the pollutions of the world through the knowledge of the Lord and Saviour Jesus Christ, they are again entangled therein, and overcome, the latter end is worse with them than the beginning.

"For it had been better for them not to have known the way of righteousness, than, after they had known it, to turn from the holy commandment delivered unto them.

"But it is happened unto them according to the true proverb, The dog is turned to his own vomit again, and the sow that was washed to her wallowing in the mire." (2 Peter 2:20-22.)

Peter is saying that what we do is not strictly our own business.

Again in our own day the Lord has said: "And now, verily I say unto you, I, the Lord, will not lay any sin to your charge; go your ways and sin no more; but unto that soul who sinneth shall the former sins return, saith the Lord your God." (D&C 82:7.)

It is easy to understand this philosophy from what we ourselves do. For example, I know of a man who borrowed $2500 from a friend. After several years of no payment, either of principle or interest, the friend offered to settle if the borrower would pay just $1000. Then the one owing the debt began to think that the entire amount he owed was $1000, and so it would have been if he had taken action. But he trifled and made excuses until finally the creditor told the debtor that if he did not accept this bargain by a certain date, he would be taken to court for the entire debt. The debtor felt that if he promised and trifled a little more, his friend would get tired and forget the whole thing. However, the creditor finally took the debtor to court and received a judgment for the amount of the former debt plus interest plus costs amounting to over $6100.

When the Lord forgives us on condition of a reformation taking place in our lives, we had better pay up and get the thing settled before the former sins are returned with compound interest and something thrown in for a penalty. The Lord said: "I, the Lord, am bound when ye do what I say; but when ye do not what I say, ye have no promise." (D&C 82:10.) Again he has said: "I command and men obey not; I revoke and they receive not the blessing." Then he pointed out our lack of reason when he said: "Then they say in their hearts: This is not the work of the Lord, for his promises are not fulfilled. But wo unto such, for their reward lurketh beneath, and not from above." (D&C 58:32-33.)

One of our greatest mistakes is that we sometimes think that life is unimportant, that what we do is our own business, and that what we do doesn't matter very much one way or another. This is not so. We are the children of God, formed in his image, endowed with his attributes, and heirs to his glory. We are being tested and proven and tried to see whether or not we will do all things whatsoever the Lord God shall command us. (See Abraham 3:25.) May we always live his commandments and follow his teachings.

Manufactured Genius

One of the greatest ambitions in human beings is that which prompts us to do well. Shakespeare describes several of the roads leading to accomplishment when he says, "Some people are born great, others acquire greatness, and others have it thrust upon them." Earl Nightingale tells the story of Mike Grost of Michigan. It is reported that at age three Michael's mother was reading a story to him when he suddenly stopped her and said, "Mommy, why don't you ever let me read to you?" To humor him, she handed him the book and he calmly read the book's text to her verbatim. At age eight he attended elementary school each morning and Michigan State University in the afternoon. He graduated from college at fifteen. He had an I.Q. somewhere above 200; in fact, it was so high that it could not be accurately pinpointed.

People who are born with such brilliant minds are not always the ones who achieve the most lasting fame. There are many examples where luck or circumstances seem to have had much to do with some particular success. Some people have been in the right place at the right time, or they have been born into the right family, or they have inherited wealth or other supposed advantages. We often say that one is a naturalborn teacher or a naturalborn salesman or a naturalborn orator. And probably no one would try to deny that there are certain natural differences in people that influence both their success and their failure.

Everyone has two personalities. One is the one that he is born with, and the other is the one he develops after he is born. No one is born with his brain already loaded with facts or know-how. No one is born with the habits of a genius already established.

111

Like so many other things, genius can be manufactured. Demosthenes, who became the greatest orator in the world, had a type of manufactured genius. He was born with a serious speech impediment that caused him all kinds of problems and embarrassment. He was so bothered by his difficulties that he went down to the seashore and for long periods he shouted to the waves with his mouth full of pebbles. Finally, after great study, labor, and effort, he became the greatest orator in the world. This was not in spite of his speech defect; rather, it was because of his speech defect. Demosthenes himself manufactured traits that put him in a class by himself.

There are cases of manufactured genius all around us, and sometimes our friends and teachers assist us in the manufacturing process. Such a person was Edith Stern, whose father set out to deliberately transform her into a genius. He began this process when she was a baby by piping classical music into her nursery twenty-four hours a day. When she was two and one half years of age she was checking books out of the public library. Of course, we are not sure what would have happened if she had not had this special attention.

Alexander Hamilton was considered to be a genius. He himself has given us his formula for how he made himself a genius. He said, "Men give me some credit for genius, but all of the genius I have lies in this: When I have a subject in mind I study it profoundly. Day and night it is before me. I explore it in all its bearings. My mind becomes pervaded with it. The result is what some people call the fruits of genius, whereas it is in reality the fruits of study and labor."

This simple formula can always be depended upon. The big questions involving success then become very personal ones, and each one of us must decide some objectives for himself. It would be helpful if we would get some definite answers to such questions as: How would you like to become a genius in your family relations? Or in doing your work? Or how would you like to be a genius in helping to carry on the work of the Lord?

The first step to any accomplishment is to believe in it. We ourselves may not always be able to determine our brain power, but we can control our enthusiasm and the power of our convictions, which is more important.

Benjamin Disraeli, the great former British prime minister, said, "Genius is the power to make continuous effort." Elbert Hubbard said, "The great secret of success is constancy of purpose." Calvin Coolidge voiced his own classic formula for gaining power when he said, "Nothing in the world can take the place of persistence. Talent will not. Nothing is more common than unsuccessful men with talent. Genius will not. Unrewarded genius is almost a proverb. Education will not; the world is full of educated derelicts. Persistence and determination alone are omnipotent." And Leonardo da Vinci underscored that miraculous power of industry that we ourselves may develop when he said, "Thou, O God, doth sell us all good things at the price of labor."

On the other hand, if one wants to be a dullard, a sloth, and a drug on society, all he needs to do is to remember and use all of the usual alibis, excuses, and rationalizing as to why he should not succeed. He may claim that industry is too tiring, or that success is too boring, or that it is unimportant. Some people are afraid that they might overwork and bring on a heart attack. However, far more people rust out than wear out. It is much more likely that someone will have a heart attack because of feelings of frustration, negativism, and guilt than from doing any well-planned, invigorating, productive work.

Ben Hogan, the great golfing champion, once said that because he couldn't outsmart his rivals, he decided he would become a champion by outworking them. That is a dependable way to excellence in any branch of our mental, social, or spiritual lives. Whatever our problems may be, we should not despair; there is one thing that everyone can be absolutely certain about, and that is that every one who is born into this world is given an enormous potential. It is not more capacity that we need most, for everyone operates far below the level of that capacity which he already has.

Studies have indicated that about 95 percent of the people whose biographies are in the *Encyclopedia Britannica* came from quite ordinary families. Each of us has deep, untapped reservoirs of ability. Don't worry about it if you don't think you were born in the gifted or genius categories; you can build up any success just as you can build up your physical body.

John the Revelator said:

"And I saw the dead, small and great, stand before God; and the books were opened: and another book was opened, which is the book of life: and the dead were judged out of those things which were written in the books, according to their works.

"And the sea gave up the dead which were in it, and death and hell delivered up the dead which were in them, and they were judged every man according to their works." (Revelation 20:12-13.)

Each of us is commanded to work out our salvation in fear and trembling before God.

You can't pick out superior salesmen or superior missionaries by giving them an I.Q. test, nor can you tell which of God's children are going to come forth in the resurrection of the just or to qualify for the celestial kingdom by their intelligence quotient. Someone has said that if Henry Ward Beecher had developed at the same rate after age thirty-five as he did from twenty-five to thirty-five, he would have been a colossus by age fifty, whereas John Wesley had his greatest period of growth between fifty and seventy.

Abraham Lincoln was unschooled and no one ever accused him of being a scholar, but he had a high quotient of honesty. He had the ability to love his fellowmen, and this and many other traits put him in the realm of genius. He was a genius in integrity and a genius in honor and a genius in righteousness. He said, "I am not bound to win but I am bound to be true. I am not bound to succeed but I am bound to live by the best light that I have. I will stand with anyone who stands right and I will part from him when he goes wrong."

What a man can do best, only he himself can determine. Where is the professor who could have taught Shakespeare or Michelangelo or Leonardo da Vinci? God has placed a vein of genius in every one of us, but each must learn to command the shaft by which we draw out the gold.

Demosthenes was not born a champion orator. Napoleon developed his own military genius. Caesar was an epileptic, yet there are many people who are presently drawing total and permanent disability benefits who are in better physical condition than Caesar was when he conquered the world. All of his life the apostle Paul was bothered by what he called a "thorn in the flesh." Beethoven was deaf. John Milton was blind. Every individual has within himself a natural inclination to do well if he will only do it.

Jesus set us a very high goal when he said, "Be ye therefore perfect, even as your Father which is in heaven is perfect." (Matthew 5:48.) God is all-knowing, all-wise, and all-powerful, and this is possible because he is also all-good. His progress is built on truth and righteousness. At one time Satan was the lightbearer, the brilliant son of the morning. He might have been called a prodigy or a heavenly genius. His prospects were magnificent, but when he let rebellion get into his life and disobeyed God, he began a downward course and was soon cast out of heaven. Because of his evil, Satan is destined to completely lose all of his power, even his power to do evil. He has already lost his happiness, his genius, and his godliness. The eternal laws of righteousness were summed up by the Creator when he said, "If thou doest well, shalt thou not be accepted? and if thou doest not well, sin lieth at the door." (Genesis 4:7.)

And so we come back to our proposition. How would you like to be a genius with your family? in your citizenship? in your employment? before God? And we repeat the thrilling fact that genius can be manufactured out of righteousness and good works.

No-Fault
Insurance

It has been said that there is nothing new under the sun, but frequently someone makes a rather startling application of some old idea we may not have thought about before. In recent years a proposal has been going around among the insurers of automobiles that has been referred to as no-fault insurance.

The traditional concept of paying the losses on automobiles that have been damaged in accidents has been to determine who caused the accident and hold him responsible. But this has not always worked successfully, because it is often difficult to determine exactly where the blame should be placed. Sometimes an accident may be the equal fault of both parties, or sometimes one may be 25 percent to blame and the other 75 percent to blame.

Some accidents are caused by change or circumstances that cannot be anticipated in advance, resulting in serious disagreements as to exactly where the fault lies, and many such arguments have turned into expensive lawsuits. There have also been cases where the expense involved in determining the liability has been greater than the cost of the damage. Then someone came up with the idea of no-fault insurance, whereby the insurer pays all of the claim without trying to determine where the blame rests.

The advantage of this kind of a procedure is that money formerly spent in expensive investigation and lawsuits can be used in paying claims no matter who is at fault. This also saves hard feelings and time, though it may encourage irresponsibility.

This may be a new and very good idea so far as paying automobile claims is concerned, but in our society the no-fault idea can hurt in many ways. It is an interesting coincidence that as our society has been deteriorating in the past few years, our irresponsibility has been increasing. Many people take refuge in the no-fault philosophy by claiming that we are all the products of our environment and there is nothing that we can do about it. Some feel that we become what our society makes us, that we ourselves are not liable and should not be asked to bear the blame.

Frequently the conflict of good and evil gets us so mixed up that we lose our sense of right and wrong. A newspaper reporter was once asked whether or not she believed in the Ten Commandments. She replied, "Who am I to say what is right or wrong?" If this young woman does not know whether or not the Ten Commandments are right, then what does she know? It is a great convenience for some people to be able to say, "What difference does it make anyway whether a thing is right or wrong?" Some people think, "I am what I am and there is nothing I can do about it." Or they just say, "I couldn't care less either one way or the other."

And so we try to alibi, offer excuses, and rationalize ourselves out of our problems. We accuse the devil or our parents or blame some experience of our childhood for our weakness. William Ernest Henley had a more

117

substantial sense of responsibility when as a hopeless cripple he wrote the poem "Invictus":

Out of the night that covers me,
    Black as the Pit from pole to pole,
I thank whatever gods may be
    For my unconquerable soul.

In the fell clutch of circumstance
    I have not winced nor cried aloud.
Under the bludgeoning of chance,
    My head is bloody, but unbowed.

Beyond this veil of wrath and tears
    Looms but the Horror of the shade,
And yet the menace of the years
    Find and shall find me unafraid.

It matters not how straight the gate,
    How charged with punishments the scroll,
I am the master of my fate:
    I am the captain of my soul.

Such a philosophy, if universally adopted, would soon transform our world into God's paradise. And the scriptures say that every individual person beyond the age of accountability must and will be held fully responsible for his works.

When we use the no-fault philosophy, we are making a serious miscalculation of fact. We can be sure that God will not have us covered with no-fault insurance. Certainly the murderer, the adulterer, the Sabbath breaker, the profane, and the criminal will not all share the same fate as the saint. God attaches a different kind of value to rebellion than he does to loyalty. Truth and falsehood, industry and sloth, courage and cowardice, heaven and hell all have different significance for us. It is difficult to live the religion of Christ if we have the attitude of the devil, but it is easy to live the religion of Christ if we have the standards and spirit of Christ. It is easy to live effectively in the world if we avoid the sins of the world. There are many inspiring examples of people who have lived in the world and yet have not been of the world.

We remember the inspirational story of the young French peasant maid, Joan of Arc. Louis Kossuth said she was the only person who ever held supreme command of a great national army at age seventeen. By the age of nineteen she had delivered France from its enemies and become the heroine of her country.

Although she lived in the most brutal and wicked period since the Dark Ages, yet she did her job as well as anyone that any nation has ever produced. She lived when crime was common among mankind. She was truthful when lying was the ordinary speech of man. She was honest when honesty was a lost virtue. She maintained her personal dignity, unimpaired, in an age of fawning and servilities. She said that even the rude business of war could be better conducted without profanity and the other brutalities of speech.

She had dauntless courage when hope had perished in the hearts of her countrymen. She was spotlessly pure in mind and body when most of society was foul in both. She was the genius of patriotism, the embodiment of sainthood, and finally wore a martyr's crown upon her head.

Few could understand why Joan continued to be alert, vigorous, and confident while her strongest men were exhausted by long marches and severe exposure. On one occasion with an almost impossible objective ahead, she said, "I will lead the men over the wall." One of her generals said, "Not a man will follow you." Joan replied, "I will not look back to see whether anyone is following or not."

Then, with a flash of her sword, she gave the signal and led the way, and the soldiers of France followed. She was often seen sweeping across the plain at the head of her troops, her silver helmet shining, her bright cape fluttering in the wind, her sacred sword flashing, her consecrated banner held aloft. With an unshakable belief in her mission glowing in her heart, she swept everything before her. She sent a thrill of courage and conviction through the French army such as neither king nor patriot could produce. Instead of developing sins and weaknesses by saying "Everybody's doing it," Joan of Arc always did what she believed to be right.

Any success is extremely difficult when we recognize no weakness or fault in ourselves. Since time began, one of our biggest problems has been caused by those people who commit many sins and then say "I am not to blame. It was not my fault." We try to solve too many of our problems by adopting a martyr's complex or imagining that everyone is picking on us. Too many people have the feeling that no matter what the situation may be, no fault attaches to them.

Recently I observed a rather horrifying example of this no-fault philosophy, which was brought to the surface in a divorce proceeding. All through his life the husband had had a lot of problems, and instead of learning to recognize them, he had tried to solve them by the traditional ostrich method of hiding his own head in the sand. He had developed a hide as thick and tough as an elephant's, so no feeling of responsibility could get through to him. When his parents had tried to counsel and advise him, he developed a persecution complex and felt that for some reason they were maliciously picking on him—this in spite of the fact that it must have been perfectly clear to all of his senses that he himself was at fault.

His wife's life since her marriage to him had been a terrible ordeal. Before her marriage she herself had had a

120

moral indiscretion, and in an attempt to clean the slate she had confessed her past sin to him before they were married. He brushed it aside as unimportant, but in the ten years that passed since then, he repeatedly brought it up to her. He himself had also been a transgressor, but all of his sins were not only forgotten by him, but they were also completely excused. It was as though his wife's past had covered him with some no-fault insurance that made all sin unblamable in him.

Few things are more difficult than to try to reason with someone whose mind is so calloused that logic is not possible. By our rejection of responsibility, we can sink others into the depths of depression or push them to the very edge of a breakdown. We therefore increase our own problems and at the same time decrease our ability to solve them.

We were placed here upon this earth to learn to overcome problems and develop our strength. One of the most certain facts in our existence is that we do not live in a no-fault world. Nothing is more clearly written in the scriptures than that we are going to be judged according to our works. There is a fundamental law in the universe that says that someday the books of our lives must be balanced. We can no more do a good thing without at some time, in some way, receiving a reward than we can do an evil thing without suffering a penalty. We should know that if we live righteously, if we develop our minds and wills and personalities, we will be rewarded. May God help us be wise enough to eliminate our faults and choose righteousness.

The Chains
of Hell

The scriptures speak a great deal about the bondage of Satan, the imprisonment of evil, the bands of death, and the chains of hell. Although these terms represent conditions that are very real and should be important to us, yet they sometimes don't influence us much because we do not fully understand what they mean.

The prophet Alma tells about some people whose souls were on the very brink of destruction when they were rescued by their own repentance. Changing their attitudes was like being awakened out of a deep spiritual sleep. They had been in the midst of thick darkness, but now their souls were illuminated by the light of the word of the Lord. Alma tries to describe the situation of these people by saying that they had been encircled by the bands of death and had been bound down by the chains of hell. Their repentance had released them from an everlasting destruction.

Since the beginning of time, men have been taken captive by the devil and have been led by him down to eternal destruction. Jude comments on a different side of this situation when he says: "And the angels which kept not their first estate, but left their own habitation, [God] has reserved in everlasting chains under darkness unto the judgment of the great day." (Jude 6.) The Lord comments on this awful situation when, in our own day, he has said: ". . . the wicked have I kept in chains of darkness." (D&C 38:5.) Many people have a tendency to enslave themselves by doing evil. The Lord says the whole world groans under the weight of its iniquity. He says that this captivity is as "an iron yoke, it is a strong band; they are the very handcuffs, and chains, and shackles, and fetters of hell." (D&C 123:8.)

A chain is a series of connected rings or links that

are usually made out of metal. Chains are used for various purposes, to encumber or restrain. There are also other kinds of chains. An engineer's chain is a means of measurement. We speak of a chain of mountains or a chain of events. A number of radio stations may join together to form a broadcasting chain. We have chain stores and chain reactions.

We also draw chains of thought out of our minds, and our emotions are linked up together in our hearts in a similar way. Thoughts almost never come singly and alone. They almost always form themselves into chains. These groups seem to have an affinity for each other as though they were tied together.

One of the important ways to learn is through association of ideas. We remember poetry or other things most easily when they have a chain of continuity tied together by meter, rhyme, and rhythm. In our relations with others, we may sometimes become chained together by our thoughts and interests. Because we are more or less chained together, we may draw each other up or drag each other down. A low-souled person who tends to think in his own level may lower our altitude. On the other hand, when we attach ourselves to high-minded people and the thoughts in inspiring literature, it is as though a great chain were let down with a grab-hook on its end to lift us upward.

When we succumb to too many low influences, we tend to feel that we are the slaves of our environment. However, we also have a godly ability for decision making and follow-through. We are completely free to choose those things which will draw us upward.

When we give way to evil we tend to respond to future evil more or less automatically until it may carry us to a point where we lose control of ourselves. Because of our weaknesses, evil power can also get power over us by default. We are all different, and rarely does one's self-control descend to a zero, or rarely does anyone have complete self-control. Therefore, our degree of control over ourselves varies according to how effectively we work at it.

Brigham Young once said: "A man can dispose of his agency or his birthright as did Esau of old. But when disposed of he cannot again obtain it. Those who dispose of the proffered mercies of the Lord have their agency immediately abridged and bounds and limits are then set upon them. When listened to, evil begins to rule and overrule the spirit which God has planted within man."

Joseph Fielding Smith pointed out that God has caused some civilizations to be destroyed as an act of mercy to those involved. Nations or peoples have become so wicked that the children growing up among them have little possibility for developing true agency; then that culture has sometimes been destroyed to break this chain of evil and give everyone a better chance.

We often see the destructive influence of a chain in operation when one takes his first drink of liquor. He may not do it because he wants to drink, but because he wants to be friendly. Someone has said that becoming an alcoholic is like getting olives out of a narrow-necked bottle. The first one may be a little difficult, but after the way has been cleared, the others come out more easily. And so it is that one drink usually calls for another, and a million future drinks may all be linked to the first one. In like manner, one cigarette may be tied to numberless other cigarettes, with lung cancer bringing up the rear.

Some people may think of preliminary sins as harmless, but they are tied to sins that can destroy our souls. Like attracts like and sin begets sin. And there is nothing about being a weakling or a coward today that will make us giants and heroes tomorrow. Betrayal inspires betrayal. Weakness begets weakness; and each link is a little larger and stronger than its predecessor. Someone has said:

It was such a little, little sin
And such a great big day,
And I thought the hours would swallow it,
Or the wind blow it away.

But the moments passed so quickly
And the wind died out somehow,
And the sin that was a weakling once
Is a hungry giant now.

We remember the story of Charles Dickens' *Christmas Carol*, where the ghost of Jacob Marley made a visit to his former partner, Scrooge, on the seventh anniversary of his death. He came up the stairs dragging a long chain of fetters made up of cash boxes and other things behind him. When asked for an explanation, Marley's ghost said, "These are the chains I forged in life."

Evil has a dangerous characteristic. Once it gets a foothold, it quickly begins crowding out righteousness. When young people start having a part in evil, they soon begin losing interest in the things they formerly treasured. Then they no longer enjoy engaging in family prayer. When they begin to smoke or drink, the Word of Wisdom offends them. They become annoyed by any discussion of those ideas that are opposed to what they are doing. The stronger the guilt complex, the more they are oppressed by good. Then they like to get as far away as possible from the restraints of good parents and teachers. Evil has a way of demanding the patronage of its devotees.

May the Lord help us to keep our lives free from the bondage of Satan and the chains of hell so that we may be governed by his laws of righteousness and inherit that glorious destiny which God himself has provided.

Dedication

The dictionary says that dedication is an act or a rite of setting apart or dedicating something to a divine being or to a sacred use. It is a solemn appropriation of values, and the dictionary gives as an example the dedication of Solomon's temple. It also points out that on November 19, 1863, the national cemetery of Gettysburg, Pennsylvania, was dedicated as the final resting place of those who fell in one of the greatest battles of the Civil War. We remember that it was on this occasion that President Abraham Lincoln gave his famous Gettysburg Address:

"Fourscore and seven years ago our fathers brought forth upon this continent a new nation, conceived in liberty, and dedicated to the proposition that all men are created equal.

"Now we are engaged in a great civil war, testing whether that nation, or any nation so conceived and so dedicated, can long endure. We are met on a great battlefield of that war. We have come to dedicate a portion of that field as a final resting-place for those who here gave their lives that that nation might live. It is altogether fitting and proper that we should do this. But in a larger sense we cannot dedicate, we cannot consecrate, we cannot hallow this ground. The brave men, living and dead, who struggled here, have consecrated it far above our poor power to add or to detract. The world will little note, nor long remember, what we say here; but it can never forget what they did here.

"It is for us, the living, rather to be dedicated here to the unfinished work which they who fought here have thus far so nobly advanced. It is rather for us to be here dedicated to the great task remaining before us, that from these honored dead we take increased devotion to that cause for which they gave the last full measure of devotion; that we here highly resolve that these dead

126

shall not have died in vain; that this nation, under God, shall have a new birth of freedom, and that government of the people, by the people, and for the people, shall not perish from the earth."

And thus this spot of ground was dedicated to God as the final resting place of those stalwart sons who had answered the call of their country and had given their lives for a sacred purpose.

Governments were instituted by God for the benefit of man, and he holds all men accountable for their acts in relation thereto. He requires that we dedicate ourselves to promote the national good, not only in time of war, but all of the time. He himself has said that when one is in the service of his fellowmen, he is also in the service of God.

God has also established his church upon the earth. He has commanded that all men should have faith in him, be baptized, and devote themselves to carrying on his work through his church organization. We build houses of worship as well as sacred temples where his work can be effectively carried on in his name.

More than three thousand years ago, David was anointed by Samuel to be the king of ancient Israel. Among other things, the people needed a temple. It had been nearly four hundred years since the Israelites had entered their promised land under Joshua, and for all of these years the only thing they had to serve them as a temple was the little portable tabernacle they carried around with them as they wandered in the wilderness.

The people needed the temple. The Lord wanted them to have a temple, and David, the king, wanted to build the temple. However, an important part of dedication is worthiness, and because David was not worthy to build the temple, the Lord said that its construction would have to wait until after David's death. Finally, after Solomon had succeeded his father upon the throne, the Lord commanded him to build that great temple to God which has been known through the ages as Solomon's temple.

This luxurious edifice required seven years to build. The altars, many parts of the building, and much of the furniture were overlaid with pure gold. The building was also beautified and ornamented with valuable gems and costly jewels. Then, when the building was completed, Solomon stood before the altar with his hands spread forth toward heaven, and the record says that he and all the people dedicated the temple unto the Lord.

After Solomon had finished his dedicatory prayer, fire came down from heaven and consumed the sacrifices. Then the Lord appeared unto Solomon by night and said, "If my people, which are called by my name, shall humble themselves, and pray, and seek my face, and turn from their wicked ways; then will I hear from the heaven, and will forgive their sin, and will heal their land." (2 Chronicles 7:14.)

For many years this temple was one of the wonders of the world. It was the symbol of Jehovah worship in the earth. It was the devotional center of Israel. But the important part of dedication is in people and not in buildings or costly ornaments, and because the people themselves did not keep the covenants they had made when they had dedicated the temple, and because they themselves failed to maintain their purpose, the temple soon began a downward course. It was shorn of much of its magnificence by invaders, and it was despoiled of its treasures by both local and foreign sinners. Some of its gold was used by the people to buy off the attacks of enemies and some was used to purchase the cooperation of other nations. Finally the temple was burned to the ground and utterly destroyed by Nebuchadnezzar, the king of Babylon, and all of those remaining treasures were carried away to Babylon. The temple was subsequently rebuilt on the same spot by King Zerubbabel, but because of the wickedness of the people, it was again destroyed. It was in the process of again being rebuilt by King Herod during the ministry of Jesus.

This historic spot had great significance in the lives of the Israelites. It was here that an angel commanded David to build an altar on which to offer a sacrifice to Jehovah. It was here that the magnificent temple of Solomon stood. It was here that Jesus himself came, and that he taught the wise men when he was twelve years of age.

Some few weeks before the crucifixion, because of the antagonism of the people, Jesus left Jerusalem and went some twenty miles to the little village of Ephraim, where he spent some time in training his apostles for the responsibilities that would soon rest upon their shoulders. Then, as the feast of the Passover approached, he startled his followers by saying, "Come, let us go into Judea again." (John 11:7.) Just seven days before he would hang with outstretched arms above Calvary, he began that solemn march toward Jerusalem and the cross. He arrived in Bethany, about a mile and a half from Jerusalem, on Friday evening, at the beginning of the Sabbath. This was the home of Mary, Martha, and Lazarus.

Over the last Sabbath (from Friday evening to Saturday evening) the Gospel writers have drawn a reverent veil of silence. Then on Sunday morning, the first day of the week, Jesus made his triumphal entry into Jerusalem riding on the back of an ass. Passover travelers from many areas were also making their way toward Jerusalem, and as he became a part of this imposing procession, palm branches and flowers were strewn in his path along the way. The people shouted, "Hosanna to the son of David: Blessed is he that cometh in the name of the Lord." (Matthew 21:9.)

All day long he taught the people in the temple without success. On Monday he returned again. This is the day when he cleansed the temple by driving out the moneychangers. He said, "It is written, My house is a house of prayer: but ye have made it a den of thieves." (Luke 19:46.) On Tuesday he came again for the last time to the temple, and all day long he taught the people, again without success. As the end of the day approached, Jesus left the precincts of the temple and began his journey back to Bethany.

As he crossed the Mount of Olives he stopped to rest near its summit and, with his followers around him, turned and looked back to the temple. Then he made his famous farewell speech to Jerusalem. He said: "O Jerusalem, Jerusalem, thou that killest the prophets, and stonest them which are sent unto thee, how often would I have gathered thy children together, even as a hen gathereth her chickens under her wings, and ye would not! Behold, your house is left unto you desolate." (Matthew 23:37-38.)

He was leaving this sacred edifice forever, and it no longer qualified as a temple of God. This is an indication of that sacred truth that the most important objects for dedication are not made from the cedars of Lebanon or the sycamore, nor are they made of gold and rubies. Rather, they are made of human lives. May we each dedicate ourselves to those sacred causes to which God himself is devoted!

An Ounce
of Prevention

If our lives are to be successful, there are certain things that must be done—and certain things that must be left undone. A fundamental law of life says that everyone must be judged according to his works. A corollary to this also says that there are certain experiences that must be prevented from taking place. We may lose our eternal exaltation by neglecting either one of these two processes. One problem is that we don't go far enough in the right direction and the other is that we go too far in the wrong direction. We must provide ourselves with sufficient motivation for the one and an adequate system of restraining power for the other. There are probably a lot more people who lose their blessings because of doing wrong than who fail to earn them by doing right.

Someone has pointed out that while there are a hundred steps from hell to heaven, there is only one from heaven to hell. It takes years to build a life, but it can be destroyed in an instant. Some time ago I listened to discussions about three men who were being considered for an appointment to office. As their virtues and vices were being compared, of each one it was said he is good in certain areas but lacking in others. I discovered that it isn't always important what one's great virtues are, because they can so easily be cancelled out by little vices. Of the first man it was said, "He is a great person and he wants the job, *but* he is lazy." Of the second it was said, "He is a great scholar, a hard worker, very ambitious, *but* he is immoral." Of the third it was said, "He is very capable, he has a fine record, he knows the business, *but* he doesn't want the job."

A banker can balance off a hundred-dollar liability with a hundred-dollar asset. But one can't do that in public relations or in leadership responsibilities. If a political candidate goes before the people with ten virtues and one little vice the people, particularly those of the opposing party, do not say, "Let's sit down and talk about his ten virtues." What they want to do is thoroughly discuss his one vice.

It is important that we build up our virtues, but it is even more important that we eliminate our vices. One wrecking crew, whether in the building trades or in life, can destroy in an hour what it has taken several lifetimes

131

to build up. We must select the right and exclude the wrong. We must center our minds on the good and then be able to effectively motivate ourselves to bring about its accomplishments.

Even greater skill is required in life to prevent from happening those things that would destroy our accomplishment. An old axiom says: "An ounce of prevention is worth a pound of cure." Many years ago a story came out of India indicating that each year 50,000 natives were crushed by pythons. The natives discovered that it was better to search out the python eggs where they had been laid in the sand and destroy them before they were hatched than to struggle with the deadly snakes after the pythons had been allowed to mature. We have innumerable examples of this idea. In 1886, 120,000 people in America lost their lives to the scourge of smallpox. Then someone invented a preventative in the form of a vaccine, and for the past several years there has not been a single death from that python of disease; we have destroyed its strength by preventing it from being born.

I received several lessons, many years ago, in the disadvantages of letting a problem develop its full strength and then trying to overcome it. When I was a small boy, my father built an irrigation reservoir on a high part of our land where water could be impounded when it was plentiful and used when it was scarce; when our irrigation turn came at night, we could put the water in the reservoir and use it during the daytime.

On one occasion it was necessary to repair the valve in the outlet. But when the pipe was put back, sufficient care was not taken to see that the dirt was made firm enough that the water could not leak through it. We learned that a little leak in the dike, if not taken care of early, could be disastrous. Then it was too late to do very much about it. For many hours the men worked feverishly, throwing in rocks and sandbags in an effort to stem the tide of waters that an hour or two before had been only a tiny wet spot on the other side of the reservoir dam. And as a result, instead of the water helping the young crops, the flood of waters rushed down through the young plants and washed out all prospects for a crop that year. A little more attention given to prevention would have guaranteed an abundant harvest.

I also remember another impressive lesson about prevention. It was my job to prevent the growth of the tall sweet clover in the orchard, and I discovered to my sorrow that if I let this tough weed get a good head start, it was very difficult to destroy its tough roots. My job would have been easy if I had gotten after it in the early spring when the ground was soft and the plants were small and tender.

To refuse those first cigarettes provides much better control of lung cancer than to try to struggle with the disease after the awful monster has been allowed to grow. Immorality is a python that has devastated many lives, destroying confidence, bringing venereal disease, breaking up families, and causing serious eternal destruction. Fear is a python. The unprofitable servant said, "I was afraid, so I hid my talent in the ground." (See Matthew 25:25.) There are many more important ways to control fear than by giving in to it.

The Lord himself said, "If ye are prepared ye shall not fear." (D&C 38:30.) We can prepare for any problem if we start working on it in time. Recently a man came to see me about his marital difficulties. A half dozen times his wife had cancelled her divorce proceedings on his promise to reform, but now her patience had become completely exhausted, so he came seeking the aid of others. He admitted all of the charges and then some. He said, "I have been unthoughtful. I have been immoral. I have done everything in the book, but now I would like to have my wife and family forgive me and start over again."

I could understand how he felt. I felt that same way when I was trying to cut that uncuttable clover. When the reservoir broke and we lost our crops I would like to have been able to put the water back into the reservoir and restore the crops that had been washed away. But it is pretty hard to repent of full-grown clover or a broken reservoir dam when the damage has already been done.

This man with the marital troubles wants to start over and that is a wonderful idea, if he can do it. But he couldn't behave himself even when his pythons were just small wiggling snakes. How can he handle them now that their giant coils are so tightly wrapped around him? If we can't carry our burdens while they are light, how are we going to manage them when their load is a hundredfold? It is much easier to control one's temper while the pythons are still eggs than to try to struggle with them after they have become pythons. The time to prepare a ship for the storm is not when the vessel is in the middle of the ocean being smashed by the waves. It is while the boat is still in the dockyard, while the planks are being picked and the rivets are being driven. It is difficult to get our children to love and respect us if their confidence has been destroyed time after time in the past. If one wants to prevent destruction, mistrust, and hate growing in the hearts of loved ones, the best time to do it is before the seeds have been allowed to germinate.

In the book of Revelation we are told of a message that the Lord sent to the members of the church at Laodicea. They had brought a harsh condemnation on themselves because they had allowed the weeds of indecision, indifference, and sloth to grow up in their hearts. The Lord said to them, "I know thy works, that thou art neither cold nor hot. . . . So then because thou art lukewarm, and neither cold nor hot, I will spue thee out of my mouth. Because thou sayest, I am rich, and increased with goods, and have need of nothing; and knowest not that thou art wretched, and miserable, and poor, and blind, and naked." (Revelation 3:15-17.)

Evil things, as well as good things, begin small. Nothing is ever born fully grown. If we learn to tell good from evil and then develop strong habits about every good thing, we soon become enthusiastic, hardworking, and build some solid habits around each individual success. But if we allow a few little leaks in the dikes of truth or if we take privileges with sin and pay no attention to the disease of immorality, we can be certain that it will grow into some kind of a vicious python or destructive flood of waters that will destroy us.

Our world is witnessing the awful spectacle of millions of people who are losing the most worthwhile things. They are being destroyed because the python eggs of dishonesty, atheism, criminality, immorality, and sloth were not destroyed before they were born. Those little sins that are merely pleasant pastimes now may cause us to lose our eternal exaltation. A little penicillin or a little industry or a little pledge of allegiance or some earnest covenants of righteousness made now may save our souls from being washed into hell. May the Lord help us with our program of prevention.

Freedom

The inspired Declaration of Independence states that all men are endowed by their Creator with certain inalienable rights and that among these are life, liberty, and the pursuit of happiness.

Freedom is one of our greatest gifts from God. The U.S. Constitution guarantees Americans freedom of speech, freedom of assembly, freedom to worship, and freedom to own property.

In 1941 President Franklin D. Roosevelt announced his famous four freedoms. It was his objective that every American should have freedom of speech, freedom of worship, freedom from want, and freedom from fear. We have the freedom to think, the freedom to grow, the freedom to love, the freedom to be loved, the freedom to raise our lives above the ordinary, the freedom to become like God.

Too often, however, men and women destroy their God-given freedom. Most of the battles ever waged have been fought in an attempt to deprive others of their freedom. This destructive program began with the war in heaven, when Lucifer wanted to establish himself as the savior of the world. He wanted to save everyone by compulsion. When his program of force and limitation was rejected, he rebelled against God and led one-third of all of the hosts of heaven after him. Ever since, he and his followers have seized every opportunity to deprive men of free agency and to enslave them.

Monarchs sometimes put mental and physical fetters on their subjects, forcing them to think and to act in certain ways. The Alexanders, the Caesars, the Napoleons, the Kaisers, the Hitlers, and the Stalins have tried many times to conquer the world and, like Lucifer, to subjugate its people. There are dictators in the world today who would without a moment's hesitation enslave everyone if they could.

World War I was said to be fought to make the world safe for democracy. That was also the avowed purpose of World War II, and that is the reason why we are spending so much in human lives and money in withstanding the spread of communism.

In his great program for the latter days, God raised up inspired men to establish the Constitution of the United States, and ordained that America's mission in the world should be to serve as the citadel of liberty and to keep freedom, righteousness, and human dignity alive. We have met with all kinds of opposition, inspired by the continued leadership of Lucifer, the fallen son of the morning.

God himself has made a strong personal commitment to freedom. He has said: "Ye shall know the truth, and the truth shall make you free." (John 8:32.)

Righteousness, good attitudes, and plenty of industry will also make us free. God has given us the lifesaving principles of the gospel to help us to keep ourselves free and happy. But in order to keep ourselves free, we must keep our minds free to think. Each of us needs a clear conscience and a will that is not fettered by bad habits or evil distortions.

In order to keep our freedom, we must place out of bounds all those things that would enslave us. James says: "Resist the devil, and he will flee from you." (James 4:7.) Sometimes people bring disaster upon themselves when they fail to distinguish between freedom and irresponsibility, not recognizing that the right kind of freedom has limitations on it. For example, freedom of the press does not give anyone the license to commit libel against his neighbor. Freedom of the seas does not give anyone a pirate's license to take the treasures of others, not does it entitle anyone to sink ships or destroy lives. A very important part of liberty consists in understanding where freedom ends and license begins.

A marriage certificate does not entitle one to ruin the success or destroy the happiness of his marriage partner. When one brings children into the world, he is not free to desert or neglect them. Actually, no one is ever given any right to do wrong. God has said, "For I the Lord cannot look upon sin with the least degree of allowance." (D&C 1:31.) He is completely bound by his own laws of righteousness. He said, "I, the Lord, am bound when ye do what I say . . ." (D&C 82:10), and when we obey the laws of God, we begin to become free as God is free.

As we obey the laws of health, we free ourselves

137

from disease. As we obey the laws of success, we free ourselves from failure. As we obey the laws of God and heaven, we free ourselves from the bonds of Satan and the torments of hell. Even Satan is not free, and sometime when he feels the full shock of the backfire of evil, he will discover he has paid a bitter price for his rebellion and sin.

In his vision of the future, John the Revelator says:

"And I saw another angel come down from heaven, having the key of the bottomless pit and a great chain in his hand.

"And he laid hold on the dragon, that old serpent, which is the Devil, and Satan, and bound him a thousand years,

"And cast him into the bottomless pit, and shut him up, and set a seal upon him, that he should deceive the nations no more, till the thousand years should be fulfilled: and after that he must be loosed a little season." (Revelation 20:1-3.)

Since his rebellion against God in the council in heaven, Satan has taken many liberties with the truth. He is the master of license, the most ardent supporter of irresponsibility, the greatest practitioner of evil. But even now he is not free to think or to love good people or to do good things or to be happy. We must not get ourselves into this situation. In *Paradise Lost,* John Milton put some words into the mouth of the Creator when he wrote:

I formed men free and free they must remain
Till they enthrall themselves.
I will not change their natures
Or revoke the high decree that hath ordained
their freedom.
They themselves ordained their fall.

And so we come back to the statement in the Declaration of Independence: "We hold these truths to

138

be self-evident: that all men are created equal; that they are endowed by their Creator with certain inalienable rights; that among these are life, liberty, and the pursuit of happiness." Life is our greatest possession, but it is made greater by our practice of freedom and by how effectively we pursue the happiness that God has ordained.

Introductions

We have an interesting custom in which on important occasions we make introductions of people. Usually before a speaker presents an important subject to an audience, the speaker himself is introduced by someone. It is thought that when the strength and accomplishments of the speaker are made known to the audience, everyone gets more out of the discussion. The introduction is very important, for it starts the program on its way.

Actually, we don't know very much about ourselves, or about life, or even about God. We need someone to introduce us to wisdom, industry, courage, and righteousness. Some people are employed for an entire working lifetime and never really understand their work or its possibilities or its consequences. Sometimes we belittle ourselves by saying, "I'm just a teacher," or "I'm just a salesman," or "I'm just a worker." Our divorce carnage may be attributed to the fact that marriage partners have never been properly introduced to those facts and responsibilities involved in marriage. What a great help it would be if each of us could get a good introduction to our parents, our children, and our spouses. We ought to know more about this world in which we live as well as that world toward which we are working. We should also know something about the opportunities all about us.

When we introduce a speaker, we frequently tell about his past and his present interests, and we sometimes attempt to predict his future. These are also some of the things we need to know about ourselves.

Someone has said that the four most important dates in a person's life are (1) the day he is born, (2) the day he gets married, (3) the day he selects his life's work, and (4) the day he dies.

Isn't it interesting that the thing that we know less about than anything else in the world is our own individual selves? You can ask a man questions about science, invention, history, or politics, and he will answer you, but if you ask him to sit down and write out an analysis of himself and tell you about his mind and soul qualities, you may not get a very good answer. Or if you ask him where he came from or what his purpose in life is or what his eternal destiny is, he will probably be silent and uncomprehending.

Someone once said to his friend, "Who do you think you are?" His friend whispered quietly to himself, "I wish I knew." It would be of the greatest help to us if we took time to discover that we are the children of God. What exciting news to know that we were created in God's own image and that we have been endowed with his attributes. And if we could have the concealing veils of mortality drawn aside and understand our antemortal accomplishments, and godly future possibilities, we would feel like falling down and worshipping before him.

Just suppose that we could have visited with Abraham as he tended his flocks out on the plains of Palestine. We might have thought of him as a rather ordinary kind of sheepherder. But if we could have known him during his antemortal estate when, because of his integrity and righteousness, he rated as one of the greatest intelligences of heaven and was chosen to stand among the noble and great in the council of God, we would probably have had a very different opinion. Or what would we think if we could look in on Abraham at this moment as he rules with God in heaven?

The apostle Paul once said that we should be careful how we entertain strangers, because some have entertained angels unawares. But all of us are continually entertaining some of the finest of the angels. Just suppose we had the right kind of introduction to those spirits that have been sent to us from God to be our own children. They were not only sent to be entertained in our homes, but they were also sent to be educated and given their characters as well. What do you think that we ought to know about their past and their present and their future? How thrilling it is for us to know that gods, spirits, angels, and men all belong to the same species, though in different degrees of righteousness and in various stages of development.

When Jesus was born in the Bethlehem stable, the innkeeper may have announced his birth to some of the other guests by saying, "It's a boy." But suppose those people who lived then had actually known who he was. There were some who watched him grow up and listened to him speak, and yet they crucified him upon the cross, and he said of them, "Father, forgive them; for they know not what they do." (Luke 23:34.) Through the scriptures God has given us an introduction to his Son when on several occasions he has said, "This is my beloved Son, in whom I am well pleased."

In a revelation to the prophet Moses, God also made a part of his speech introducing his First Begotten Son in the spirit who was to be his Only Begotten Son in the flesh when he said to Moses, "And worlds without number have I created; and I also created them for mine own purpose; and by the Son I created them, which is mine Only Begotten." (Moses 1:33.) Yet we sometimes

141

say of him, as did the ancients, "His blood be upon us, and on our children." (Matthew 27:25.)

Consider the importance of that day when we are married. That is when God entrusts into our hands the responsibility for establishing the most important institution in the world, the home—our home. As a place to spend the first part of their lives, our first parents, Adam and Eve, were placed in the Garden of Eden. That ought to be the atmosphere of every one of our homes, for every home serves not only as a reception center, but also as a training school for immortal souls, and we serve as their teachers and examples. It is God's purpose that in our homes they should learn love, kindness, righteousness, and obedience. This is the place where the foundation of their immortality will be laid.

Our children's lives should not be exposed to bickerings and sin. They should never be faced with the ugly spectres of hate and divorce. If we were properly introduced to our wives and our children, we would certainly not allow ourselves that awful privilege of breaking their spirits, making them unstable, and causing the destruction of their chances for eternal glory.

Now for the third important day of our lives. We need a better introduction to that part of the work of the world that life has given us to do. Elbert Hubbard once said that business is the process of ministering to human needs. "Therefore," said he, "business is essentially a divine calling." That is, the farmer who provided the food for your family's breakfast this morning was ministering to a human need, and therefore he is entitled to say that he is engaged in a divine occupation. The doctor who gave me blood transfusions was ministering to a human need, and he also is employed in a divine calling. We should think of our part of the work of the world in that way and do it in that spirit. We can give ourselves the finest introduction to our work by doing it in the best way that it can be done.

The fourth most important date of our lives is the date of our deaths. In fact, someone has said that death is the most important event in life. We live to die, and then we die to live. And if we are true and faithful in this life, God will someday introduce us into the celestial kingdom, and, with his hand on our shoulder, we may hear him say, "Well done, thou good and faithful servant: thou hast been faithful over a few things, I will make thee ruler over many things: enter thou into the joy of thy lord." (Matthew 25:21.) God bless us that this may come to pass.

Downhill

An old fable tells about a farmer hauling his produce to market in a wagon drawn by two horses. The horses were having a difficult time on the steep grade. Finally the farmer said to a stranger, "How far is it to the top of the hill?" The stranger replied, "You're not on a hill, your rear wheels are off."

This farmer may seem unobserving, and yet we often fail to observe ways to make our lives easier. Jesus said: "Take my yoke upon you, . . . For my yoke is easy, and my burden is light." (Matthew 11:29-30.) But we frequently add some difficulty factors to life that are unnecessary along the narrow-road concept of success taught by Jesus. Alcoholism, idleness, nicotine-ism, dishonesty, immorality, and dope addiction make life more difficult and much more unpleasant.

The first part of my walk to work is uphill. Then, when I turn to an easy downhill grade, the walking is much more pleasant and a lot easier. Sometimes a gentle breeze blows at my back and gives me an additional lift. With good, strong conviction we can give ourselves a tail wind. Effective know-how and a little enthusiasm can make our course downhill all the way.

Nothing gives us such a good, strong, helpful tail wind as a positive mental attitude. And nothing sets the grade in our favor like some firm decisions for righteousness. But many people believe that it is too difficult to live the religion of Christ, to be successful, and to be happy. We listen to the propaganda of failure without deciding what is right or wrong. We are getting on the broad road and then taking off our rear wheels.

Recently a young man was trying to find someone to help him solve his problems. He was unemployed, and he seemed to think that to destroy the "establishment" was the first and greatest commandment. He had an untidy, dirty personal appearance and dressed in the full uniform of rebellion. He had been divorced twice, and he hated his parents. He had no money, no friends, and no desire to change himself. He was headed uphill.

We can give ourselves a downhill grade by living the golden rule. Industry and motivation can lubricate our machinery and make our lives more exciting. A social worker was once making a survey in a so-called underprivileged neighborhood. He stopped at the door of a house, and after knocking several times a small crack opened in the door and out of the inside darkness a woman's voice said, "You don't need to stop here. Me and my husband, we ain't interested in nothing." These people were carrying a heavy load of inactivity and unsociability and it must have seemed to them to be an uphill climb.

To give the journey through life a downhill grade, get up early enough to watch the sun rise. It is exciting to experience the light, warmth, and energy that helps to make the earth beautiful with flowers and vegetation.

Add momentum to the downhill course by getting excited about your work. Edward Everett Hale once said that the best education is to be perpetually thrilled by life. We should fall in love with what we are doing and learn to do it well. A salesman who loves his job has more fun and makes more sales than the salesman who hates his job.

The downhill grade will be more rewarding if you strive for excellence and recognize the satisfaction that comes from doing good. Sir Galahad said:

My good blade carves the casques of men,
My tough lance thrusteth sure,
My strength is as the strength of ten
Because my heart is pure.

We can whip up a tail wind by following the Lord's law of health and by eliminating nicotine, alcohol, caffeine, negative thoughts, criticisms, and evil from our lives.

May we make our lives easier by traveling the straight and narrow road after we give it a downhill grade and put the wind at our backs.

Liberation

We hear a great deal today about the liberation of women. We are all aware of the fact that for many years women were not permitted to get an education, nor were they allowed to vote, hold political office, or speak in public. Even the Bible has been interpreted by some as placing women in an inferior position to men. In some earlier periods daughters were not allowed to inherit property if there were any sons in the family. And only in 1919 was an amendment made in the Constitution of the United States permitting women to vote.

Women are not the only ones who have had

liberation problems. A little over a hundred years ago Americans were fighting a destructive civil war that was to decide whether or not slaves should be liberated. Present-day blacks claim that their political liberation does not satisfy them, and they are now undertaking an energetic campaign aimed at several kinds of economic and social liberation.

In a sense, everyone is serving in some kind of bondage, and everybody is attempting to get himself liberated from something. The Revolutionary War was a war to free Americans of taxation without representation. Labor unions today are trying to get their members liberated from what they think of as long hours and low pay. Eastern European nations are seeking liberation from the Communists. The Indians and other minority groups are working on programs of liberation. The Jews want to be liberated from persecution; the Catholics and Mormons would like to be liberated from religious discrimination. Millions of people who live on government relief want to be liberated from the unpleasant effects of poverty, unemployment, and work itself.

The dictionary says that liberation means to release from restraint or bondage. To liberate is to set someone free. The dictionary also mentions other kinds of liberation, such as to liberate the mind from prejudice, or to free the body from disease, or to liberate the soul from the bondage of sin.

The primary purpose of religion is to liberate us from ignorance and sin. Jesus was our greatest liberator; he said, "Deliver us from evil." He gave us the law of repentance to liberate us from the consequences of our sins. And yet we have a tendency to enslave ourselves. This has been going on for a long time. It started in the grand council in heaven, long before this earth itself was created. In the very beginning, God made a personal and solid commitment to freedom. In fact, next to life itself, free agency is his primary gift to us. And in this great commission he said to us, "Nevertheless, thou mayest choose for thyself."

In the plan of God designed for our eternal progression, it was necessary that we become mortal and live here upon this earth to acquire the bodies of flesh and bones that in the resurrection will go with us throughout eternity. In our antemortal life we walked by sight. We came here to learn to walk a little way by faith. This is the place where we are tested and proven and tried. For our development and progress a world of opposites has been prepared, so we can see good and evil side by side. God has also given us the companion law of responsibility, whereby we must suffer the consequences of any unrighteousness.

In God's plan, a Savior was to be provided to come here and redeem us from our sins on condition of our repentance. Because of our free agency, it was evident that some would be lost. Therefore, Lucifer, the brilliant son of the morning, suggested that he come here and use force and save everyone by compulsion. When his suggestion for enslavement was rejected he rebelled against God and drew away one-third of the hosts of heaven after him. And ever since that time he and his evil forces have gone up and down the earth doing what they can to enslave as many people as possible in every conceivable way. Satan is practicing a program of liberation that works against our interests. Through his program he is seeking to liberate us from those restraints of the Ten Commandments. He is stirring up people to object to the religion of Christ.

Many people today want to be released from the necessity of working for what they get. Many would rather get their bread by stealing or by legislation or by going on relief. The forces of evil are building up a great avalanche of divorce, where people are relieved from the responsibilities and restraints of marriage.

One of the greatest commands ever given by God was when he said to our first parents, "Multiply and replenish the earth, and subdue it." He has given us the privilege of bringing his spirit children into the world, where they can enjoy the magnificent benefits of mortality. As a part of this program, God made the family the greatest of all institutions. In the family is where the foundations are laid for love and happiness. God himself said, "It is not good for man to be alone." And he might have said that it is not good for women to be alone, and it is not good for children to be alone. Men and women and children were not only built to live together and to support and love each other, but it was also designed that they should be dependent upon each other.

The Declaration of Independence refers to the fact that all people are equal before the law. However, they are not equal in their life expectancy, since the average woman lives several years longer than the average man. Men and women are not spiritually equal; women were given a finer spiritual sense so that they might more effectively mold the soft clay in the lives of children. Napoleon was once asked, "What is the greatest need of France?" He gave his famous one-word answer: "Mothers." Good mothers are far more in demand now than they were in Napoleon's day. The mother was created by God to be the heart of the home. What a tragedy it is when so many women want to be like men! It is, of course, necessary for many women to be the breadwinners as well as the mothers of a family. And because of the shortage of good men, and because of the custom of older men marrying younger women, many women must remain unmarried in this life. But the traditional role of a true mother still ranks far above adopted occupations of women. Men are born with greater physical stature and more strength than women, because God intended that they should serve a different

148

function. But most women are superior to men in their ability to love and train young children to be good citizens, and the fact that some of them have liberated themselves from their godly role of training children and inspiring men to righteousness is one of the reasons for the serious worsening that has recently taken place in our society. There are a lot of women and men who are running away from life and the particular responsibilities God has given them.

Oscar Wilde once said that if God wished to punish us, all he would need to do would be to answer our prayers. If all our prayers were answered, most people would work less and get more. If the prayer of the "vocal minority" speaking for modern women's liberation were answered, we would have more rights that were wrong. We would have more dependable methods of birth control, easier divorces, more readily available abortions, fewer mothers, fewer children, and less righteousness.

How fortunate it was that the mothers of Moses, the apostle Paul, Jesus, and Abraham Lincoln were not abortionists or hung up on the latest methods of birth control. The greatest need of our world is not for more doctors nor for more lawyers nor for more bank presidents. It is for more and better wives and mothers!

Someone has said, "We admire the artist who presents mimic man upon the canvas. We applaud the sculptor who carves that same image in the enduring marble, but oh how insignificant are these achievements, though the highest and fairest in all the realms of art, as compared to the great vocation of the human mother. She works not upon canvas that will fade or upon marble that will crumble into dust, but upon mind and spirit that will endure forever and bear throughout eternity the noble impress of a mother's hand."

The mothers of the ancient scriptures felt that the greatest misfortune that could come upon them was the curse of barrenness. And I suppose that the torments of hell will have no more meaning for anyone than for those female souls who have been successful in getting themselves liberated from fulfilling their God-given privilege of bringing children into the world.

Therefore, we might go back in our imagination to that early morning of creation when God created man in his own image, "in the image of God created he him; male and female created he them. And God blessed them, and said, Be fruitful, and multiply, and replenish the earth, and subdue it. . . ." (Genesis 1:27-28.) And we might join with the Creator and say to those noble spirits who are the mothers and wives and children of men, "God bless you in the great responsibility that you have to love and train and lift the children of God up to the high level of godliness."

Woman's Search for Happiness

In recent years we have been hearing and reading a great deal about women and their search for happiness. Over the ages women were sometimes referred to in such terms as the "weaker sex" or as "unfinished men." Now many of them belong to what we might call the discontented sex. In past generations they were not permitted to vote, and their educational and occupational privileges were also somewhat limited. Many women have felt that they were being treated like second-grade citizens who were inferior to men in their political rights and vocational opportunities.

Certainly women are different from men. They do not have the physical strength or some of the other capabilities of men. On the other hand, women are superior to men in many ways. They are prettier than men; they usually live longer than men, and they have different aptitudes than men. Over the centuries men were traditionally the drunkards, the lawbreakers, the murderers, and the adulterers, whereas the traditional role of women was that of the mothers of men, the teachers of men, the inspirers of men, and the helpmeets of men.

There can be no question but that men have sometimes taken some unfair advantages of women. The Lord himself has said to the discredit of men, "We have learned by sad experience that it is the nature and disposition of almost all men, as soon as they get a little authority, as they suppose, they will immediately begin to exercise unrighteous dominion." (D&C 121:39.) In many cases in the past as well as in the present, women have been and are being made the victims of this very serious male sin of unrighteous dominion. Now a large and militant group of women are raising a cry, demanding to be liberated. They want equal political rights, equal job opportunities, and equal pay with men. Many women want more sexual independence, safer methods of birth control, easier abortions, with equal privileges to enjoy the sins that in the past were largely the domain of men.

In my youth I never heard of such a thing as a woman smoking cigarettes or drinking liquor. Women also had higher standards of morality. However, many women are now not only demanding equal opportunities in the businesses and in the professions, but they also want to dress like men, look like men, and act like men. They are also narrowing the gap between men and women in their moral standards and criminal activities.

Abraham Lincoln's mother was never permitted to vote, but her son said of her, "All that I am or ever hope to be, I owe to my angel mother." As men have taken this attitude toward women, it has made the men themselves much better. However, when men lose respect for women or think of them as imitation men, then both men and women are in serious trouble.

The fact that the women of ancient Athens did not meet with men in the marketplace was no sign that either were not doing their jobs effectively. It was not in politics or athletic games or business or war where women were supposed to excel. Women were designed to be the heart of the home. They have been given some great personal and spiritual endowments that make them far superior to men as mothers.

The biggest job in the world is that of establishing morality and teaching principles of truth and righteousness, and women will probably never be happy if they abandon this natural role and attempt to compete with men. However, they can excel as wives, home builders, trainers of children, and the inspirers of men. As a group and as individuals, women have made tremendous contributions in our world.

Anthropologist Margaret Mead wrote an article some time ago that appeared in the *Chicago Daily News*. It was entitled "The American Woman—A Sad Success Story." She said:

"The American woman is the envy of women throughout the world. She is envied for her freedom to come and go, travel alone and far away, drive a car, go to college and have an abundant choice of what she will wear, how she will furnish her home, and what she will feed her family. She is envied for her opportunity to become a lawyer, a doctor, a businesswoman or a senator, to own and manager her own property, to marry without asking the consent of her guardians and to live alone if she chooses.

"The American woman, however, presents a curious echo of what the world thinks of her. She will often say: 'I ought to be perfectly happy, I have a devoted husband, a lovely home, many friends, three delightful children, and yet. . . .'

"The sentence usually ends in some self-criticism of one sort or another. 'Why am I not happy? What is wrong with me? I know there ought to be something I could do about it.' "

For all of their material blessings and unparalleled opportunities, most women are not as happy as they ought to be. One reason may be because their own standards are unrealistic. Whether one is a woman or a man, no one can succeed in all things at the same time. It is generally unrealistic to want to be successful and happy as a mother, a homemaker, and a wife, and at the same time win laurels in the business world. Neither can one practice birth control or favor abortion and at the same time please God, whose greatest command was for woman to multiply and replenish the earth.

But even so, those women who are interested in women's liberation do not usually compare themselves with their neighbors or their own family members. Instead, they compare themselves with the women they see on television and in the newspapers and the magazines. They compare themselves with those whose hair is always beautifully groomed, whose kitchens are always spotless, whose children are well fed and well behaved, whose homes are beautiful and designed with the latest equipment. Against such measures of status, no woman, no matter how fortunate or how beautiful or how much loved, no matter how well read, trusted by her children, and adored by her husband, can ever consider herself a complete success or as completely happy. Her standards are unrealistic. She thinks she should be much more than she is and have more than she has.

In woman's search for happiness, she will be more likely to succeed if she makes her quest in that area where God placed her to function: as the heart and spirit and the motivating power of the home.

4

BUILDING WISDOM INTO OUR SOULS

"Therefore whosoever heareth
these sayings of mine, and doeth them,
I will liken him unto a wise man,
which built his house
upon a rock."

Wisdom Hath Builded Her House

Solomon reminds us of the seven pillars of wisdom: "Wisdom hath builded her house, she hath hewn out her seven pillars." (Proverbs 9:1.) Building is one of the most important occupations of man, and among the most important objects of our building are the houses we build.

Jesus tells about a wise man who built his house upon a rock. The record says:

"Therefore whosoever heareth these sayings of mine, and doeth them, I will liken him unto a wise man, which built his house upon a rock:

"And the rain descended, and the floods came, and the winds blew, and beat upon that house; and it fell not: for it was founded upon a rock.

"And every one that heareth these sayings of mine, and doeth them not, shall be likened unto a foolish man, which built his house upon the sands:

"And the rain descended, and the floods came, and the winds blew, and beat upon that house; and it fell: and great was the fall of it." (Matthew 7:24-27.)

We build houses to shelter us from the storms of life. We build houses of worship. The apostle Paul mentioned another important building situation when he said, ". . . ye are God's building. . . [Therefore] let every man take heed how he buildeth. . . ." (1 Corinthians 3:9-10.) Some buildings fall because they are built on unsure foundations; others collapse because they are insufficiently pillared.

We might follow Solomon's interesting formula and get wisdom to build us a house that is invulnerable. He does not tell us which seven pillars he had in mind, but inasmuch as it is our own house we are building, we might appropriately select the seven that would best suit us, for God himself said, "Thou mayest choose for thyself." Therefore, if we were going to exercise wisdom, what would our seven pillars be?

We might be cautioned by the fabled buildings of the Three Little Pigs, who tried to protect themselves from their archenemy, the Big Bad Wolf. One built his house of straws and another of sticks. These both shared the fate of the New Testament story of the house built upon the sand, for both went down before the puffs of the wolf. The result was that both of these little pigs were eaten up by their enemy. But the third little pig was wise enough to provide a better foundation and stronger pillars; he built his house of bricks. As a consequence, his life was saved and his enemy destroyed.

If we take up where the Three Little Pigs and the two house builders in the New Testament left off, where shall we begin? Jesus made love one of the principal pillars of the church itself. Certainly we ought to love God; we ought to love our neighbors; we ought to love our spouses; we ought to love ourselves. Therefore, love could well be the first pillar.

The number of pillars needed is seven, and inasmuch as we are given our absolute freedom to choose without limitations, what will we select for the other six?

As pillar number two, what could be better than to have the virtue and power of truth? It is indestructible and all powerful. A poet said,

Truth crushed to earth shall rise again,
The eternal years of God are hers.
But error wounded writhes in pain
And dies among her worshippers.

A life built on truth would make us very secure and give us great pride in our building.

As pillar number three, we might support our life's

house with industry. What a thrilling opportunity it is to be able to work. The primary consideration of our lives even on judgment day will be given to our works. Next to my belief in God, I believe in labor. During the Savior's ministry he repeatedly admonished his followers to be doers of his word. Just as one of the seven deadly sins is sloth, so one of the seven cardinal virtues is industry. Happy is he who makes this godly trait an integral part of his life's building!

As pillar number four we might select a powerful faith. Faith is the chief support of every accomplishment. It is the moving cause of all action. We are told that all things are possible to him that believeth.

As pillar number five, we might select freedom. We fought the war in heaven to preserve this priceless pillar of agency. The slave never rises substantially because he does things under the lash, but we may do things because of sheer love and enthusiasm. Emerson said, "Of what avail is plow or sail, or land or life, if freedom fail?" We should, however, keep in mind that freedom is not free. It must be deserved and won and continuously maintained. It is not a gift; it is an accomplishment. It is not bestowed; it is a hard-won technique. It does not abide; it must be maintained.

For pillar number six, what could make wisdom's house more attractive than those godly character qualities with which we were endowed when it was said, "And God created man in his own image." But even these godly traits were given us originally only as possibilities to be developed. Every man has two creators—God and himself. Certainly the creation of man is not something that was finished in the Garden of Eden. It is still going on. We ourselves are creators, and we may develop godly qualities to the limit.

As our seventh pillar, we must have a program, a godly way of life. We must have a connection with the source of all intelligence and power. We must be in tune with the infinite. Thomas Carlyle once said that a man's religion is the most important thing about him; that is what he thinks about and believes in and stands for and works at and lives by. How thrilling it is if we make up our minds we will live by every word that proceeds forth from the mouth of God. As the psalmist reminds us, "Except the Lord build the house, they labour in vain that build it. . . ." (Psalm 127:1.)

If we have all seven pillars, we have a completeness. However, if we leave any one of them out, we are as sounding brass and tinkling symbol. A godly way of life requires obedience to the Creator. With godly qualities of character fully developed, we may become even as God is.

We remember the story by Dr. Goodell about a house that was built upon the traits of dishonesty and irresponsibility. This account tells of a wealthy man in whose home lived a young woman to whom the entire family was devoted. She was courted and finally married by a young building contractor. Then the wealthy man engaged the contractor to build a house for him. He had a renowned architect draw the plans. Then, laying the plans before the builder, he said he wanted him to construct the finest house of which he was capable; money was no object. Everything must be of the highest quality.

However, the builder had a little dishonesty in his heart. Thinking to make an extra profit, he built a cheap foundation. He used a poor grade of lumber where he thought it would not be noticed. He adulterated the paint and slurred over the plastering. He used imitation materials for the roofing.

When the young man handed over the keys of the finished building to his wealthy benefactor, he was told that this house was his wedding present. Not long after the young couple moved in, the inferior foundation began to crack, and the rains seeped through the roof and discolored the walls. Throughout the rest of their lives, the builder and his family were continually reminded of his dishonesty. What a different house he would have built had he known that he was going to spend the rest of his life in it!

Each of us is presently building the house in which we are going to spend eternity. While we are thinking about the immortality of the body, we should also give a little thought to the immortality of the soul. If we are forced to spend eternity thinking about our own misspent lives, then we may understand a little more clearly what Paul meant when he said, ". . . let every man heed how he buildeth. . . ." Edwin Markham gives voice to this thought in these words:

We are all blind until we see
That in the human plan,
Nothing is worth the building
That does not build the man.

Why build these cities glorious
If man unbuilded goes?
In vain we build the world
Unless the builder also grows.

The Creation
of Man

When God created the body of man out of the dust of the ground, the spirit that he placed in him to guide and direct and animate the body was one that already had a long antemortal experience behind it. Our intelligent spirits had long looked forward to the creation of this earth and to being added upon with the benefits of mortality. Looking forward to our second estate, God said to those who were associated with him in the ruling councils of heaven, "We will go down, for there is space there, and we will take of these materials, and we will make an earth whereon these may dwell; And we will prove them herewith to see if they will not do all things whatsoever the Lord their God shall command them. And they who keep their first estate shall be added upon; . . . and they who keep their second estate shall have glory added upon their heads for ever and ever." (Abraham 3:24-26.)

In giving the first and primary law of life, God said to man, ". . . thou mayest choose for thyself." (Moses 3:17.) Our first and probably our most important law of life is free agency. We came here under the promise of free agency.

God left man himself unfinished and provided that man might be an important part in determining what he himself should become. What we become is up to us and will depend largely upon what we ourselves do about it.

Abraham Lincoln once turned down a postmaster because he didn't like his looks. The sponsoring senator said, "But you can't hold that poor man responsible for his face." President Lincoln said, "Every man is responsible for his face." And everyone is responsible for every other part of himself. What we are on the inside shapes our appearance on the outside, and what we are on the outside gets into our insides. Suppose you look at somebody in the moment of rage. His face becomes distorted as though he were insane. After the rage is passed, the face tends to go back to its natural position; yet, the return trip is never quite complete. When you overbend a piece of steel or overstretch an elastic, it never goes completely back to its original position.

We have all seen plain people who have become beautiful by the working of a radiant spirit. A godly spirit will make the plainest body beautiful. Great mental and spiritual traits transform our body into their likeness. Emerson once said that beauty is the mark that God sets on virtue. By what we do, we not only create our outward beauty of expression, but also virtues that shine out of the depths of our souls.

The apostle Paul indicated what the end result of our pattern of activities would be when he told the Corinthians that in the resurrection of the dead there were three primary kingdoms or glories or classifications of people. The highest is called the celestial, which Paul likened in its glory to the brightness of the sun. The second is the terrestrial, which he compared to the light of the moon. The third is the telestial, which he likened to the twinkle of a tiny star. Then Paul said: ". . . for one star differeth from another star in glory. So also is the resurrection of the dead." (1 Corinthians 15:41-42.)

Some time ago in western Canada, I thought I discovered what it would be like to ride in a telestial automobile. A missionary took me to one of my appointments in an automobile he had purchased two years previously for sixty dollars. Before we had gone very far, I noticed that smoke was coming out of both the front and the rear of this machine, and I heard noises that I had never before identified with an automobile. When we arrived at our destination, I was very pleased that the experience had been concluded satisfactorily. It then occurred to me that it would not be too inconvenient if, for the rest of my life, every time I used an automobile it was the telestial variety. But I would not like to spend an eternal life with a telestial body or a telestial mind or a telestial personality, especially when God has entrusted me to create whatever I will out of my own life.

The apostle Paul wrote to the Hebrews and explained to them how through their righteousness they might obtain a better resurrection. And what a great idea that is! In this life we may build for ourselves a stronger body, a more effective mind, a more sparkling personality. But our creative powers do not stop there. We may raise ourselves far above the telestial or the terrestrial and become celestial beings. This is a difficult idea almost totally impossible to comprehend. As the apostle Paul said to the Corinthians, "Eye hath not seen, nor ear heard, neither have entered into the heart of man, the things which God hath prepared for them that love him." (1 Corinthians 2:9.) We can imagine beauty, comfort, and success worth billions of dollars, but we cannot even conceive of the most ordinary of God's blessings to us.

President David O. McKay once said that the purpose of the gospel is to change people, to make bad men good and good men better. Evil activities reverse these processes and may make good men bad and bad men worse. But one thing is certain, and that is that every day we are being modified to our advantage or our condemnation, and those important forces going in both directions are fashioning us in their own image according to which one we give ourselves to. The scriptures looked forward to our possible destiny and said, "Ye are gods; and all of you are children of the most High." (Psalm 82:6.) The greatest work that any of us will ever do will be that of creating our own selves, and we will determine in all details the kind of people that we will become. May God bless us that because of our workmanship our eternal lives will be filled with beauty, success, happiness, and eternal glory.

What Do You Want to Be When You Grow Up?

Since time began, one of the most common questions asked of children is, "What do you want to be when you grow up?" We are accustomed to making a lot of mistakes when we are young. Childhood is a time to have fun while we prepare ourselves for the future. During childhood, many people try to help us solve our problems because in many ways we live below the level of responsibility. Even after we become of legal age, we sometimes fail to display many of the earmarks of wisdom or maturity. The rate of our maturity may depend partially upon how we answer this question, "What do you want to be when you grow up?" And there are some related questions we might also ask: What do you want to know? How do you want to feel? Whom do you want to associate with? What do you want to do?

In spite of the opportunities and advantages of our day, it is interesting that many people never actually grow up. Some reach an educational, spiritual, or social level early in life from which they never seem to advance substantially. Frequently people are no wiser at thirty than they were at twenty. They are not any happier at forty than they were at thirty. Sometimes one's character is no better at fifty than it was at forty. And many are frequently no more godly at seventy than they were at sixty.

We remember James M. Barrie's little character named Peter Pan. When Peter Pan was young he heard his parents discussing what they wanted him to do when he grew up, and because he didn't want to do these things, he decided not to grow up at all. Instead he ran away from home to live with the fairies in Never-Never Land. As a consequence, he always remained a child.

However, stagnation and retardation are not the most desirable states to be fostered in anyone's life. In God's great plan of evolution it was projected that we should pass from one state of accomplishment to another and from one estate to another until we arrived at our fullest development and our greatest glory where we have the fullest enjoyment of the finest faculties and the most godly abilities.

The apostle Paul spoke of this growing-up process when he said: "When I was a child, I spake as a child, I thought as a child: but when I became a man, I put away childish things." (1 Corinthians 13:11.) We must not cling too long to our childishness or by such retarding activities that we become permanent victims of that dread disease known as arrested development.

Ethel Barrymore, the actress, was once criticizing actor Douglas Fairbanks, Jr., and someone said to her, "But Ethel, he is so young." Miss Barrymore replied, "Yes, but he has been so young so long."

Solomon devised a kind of timetable for the important journey toward maturity when he said, "To every thing there is a season, and a time to every purpose under the heaven: A time to be born, and a time to die; a time to plant, and a time to pluck up that which is planted." (Ecclesiastes 3:1-2.) Then he went on to delineate a long list of things that should be done on a regular, predetermined schedule.

We might add something to Solomon's list and say, "There is a time to develop character qualities and a time to build faith. There is a time to mature a strong personal self-control in order to improve all of our life's situations. Early in life is a time to throw away bad temper and childish irresponsibilities so that we can practice those great virtues of human maturity at their best."

God called Abraham the "father of the faithful," and he promised to make of Abraham's posterity the greatest nation on the earth. After they were released from their

Egyptian bondage, God met the Israelites before Mount Sinai and gave them the Ten Commandments to help them mature spiritually. But like Peter Pan, there were many of these things that they did not want to do. When we grow up we must exchange our ignorance for understanding.

To hand the control of our lives over to bad temper, irresponsibility, lying, cheating, profanity, rebellion, coveting, and killing will continue to keep us retarded. All sinners are trying to solve their problems by immature means. Child marriages are never successful if there is insufficient maturity to maintain happiness at a high level. Before anyone takes upon himself the responsibility of marriage and parenthood, he ought to make sure that he has a good supply of religious, financial, emotional, and personality maturity. With maturity one is no longer free to indulge his own childish whims and fancies.

Recently I talked with a mother of seven children who had some serious marital problems. She had become bored with her husband, and instead of correcting the problems in an adult way, she became infatuated with another man. Instead of being guided by what was right, she was impelled by her unrighteous appetites to meet clandestinely the object of her new interest. The result was moral transgressions serious enough to break up two families, which will undoubtedly have very serious consequences in the lives of many people. Her wonderful children have been humiliated and embarrassed by the childish actions of their mother, who is performing on a much lower standard of maturity than are the children themselves.

Some people can be faithful only when no temptation is present. They can practice maturity only by fits and starts, whereas Jesus was speaking of a more grown-up person when he said, ". . . he that endureth to the end shall be saved." (Matthew 10:22.) Elbert

Hubbard also mentioned this character quality when he said, "The secret of success is constancy of purpose." Disraeli said, "Genius is the power to make continuous effort."

I know of a man who is continually going stale in his occupation. He cannot maintain his interest in his work. He starts a new job with his enthusiasm at the top of the thermometer, but as soon as he discovers that the job has a few problems to work out and some disadvantages to endure, his enthusiasm gradually declines until his job has lost most of its attraction and challenge. His ambition cannot be maintained in the presence of problems, and so he abandons each job in turn and starts over, only to repeat the failure cycle in some other place.

Now we might ask ourselves, What about maturity and eternal life? Of course, we are aware that mortality is not the end of existence. Neither is this the place where our finest and most glorious objectives are finally realized. Someone pointed out our problem when he said, "Seeing we are here but for a day's abode, we must look elsewhere for an eternal resting place where eternity is the measure, felicity the state, angels the company, the Lamb is the Light, and God is the portion and inheritance."

It has been said that our pre-earth existence is the childhood of our immortality and that this life is the time when we grow up. In the interest of our own eternal maturity, we might again ask ourselves, What do we want to be when we grow up? With whom will we want to be associated? What relationship will we have to have with God?

The scriptures indicate that if they follow the saving laws of righteousness, the offspring of God may become even as their eternal parents. What a great disappointment it will sometime be for those who have followed Satan to discover that their progress has been eternally stopped and that all of the good has been smothered out of their lives! And what a great disappointment it will be for us if someday we find that we have arrived at a place where we did not want to go, and that we have become what we did not want to be! Jesus said, "Be ye therefore perfect, even as your Father which is in heaven is perfect." (Matthew 5:48.) And we *can* be perfect if we will.

The Family

By nature God designed human beings to be gregarious, and they always do better when they live and work harmoniously together in governments, businesses, social groups, the church, and the family. In our world no one lives successfully unto himself alone.

The family was designed as the chief source of our education, our love, our security, our prosperity, and our happiness. In the very beginning, God said, "It is not good for man to be alone," and he might have said, "It is not good for women to be alone, and it is not good for children to be alone."

The scriptures tell of the elaborate creation that took place when God brought into being this productive, beautiful earth to serve as our home. The crowning scene took place on the sixth day when God placed man upon the earth.

Recently someone was criticizing the scriptures, saying that the book of Genesis gives two conflicting accounts of creation. Many people are confused because they do not understand that the account in the first chapter of Genesis describes our spiritual or pre-earth creation. This account is as follows:

"And God said, Let us make man in our image, after

our likeness: and let them have dominion over the fish of the sea, and over the fowl of the air, and over the cattle, and over all the earth, and over every creeping thing that creepeth upon the earth.

"So God created man in his own image, in the image of God created he him; male and female created he them.

"And God blessed them, and God said unto them, Be fruitful, and multiply, and replenish the earth, and subdue it: and have dominion over the fish of the sea, and over the fowl of the air, and over every living thing that moveth upon the earth." (Genesis 1:26-28.)

While this creation of men, women, and all other things took place in heaven, it looked forward to the great drama of our mortal existence. This account of the creation of our spirits is reviewed and explained in the second chapter when the Lord says:

"These are the generations of the heavens and of the earth when they were created, in the day that the Lord God made the earth and the heavens,

"And every plant of the field before it was in the earth, and every herb of the field before it grew: for the Lord God had not caused it to rain upon the earth, and there was not a man to till the ground.

"And there went up a mist from the earth, and watered the whole face of the ground.

"And the Lord God formed man of the dust of the ground, and breathed into his nostrils the breath of life; and man became a living soul." (Genesis 2:4-7.)

The Lord makes this scripture clearer as it is recorded in some ancient writing of Moses not found in the Bible:

"And every plant of the field before it was in the earth, and every herb of the field before it grew. For I, the Lord God, created all things, of which I have spoken, spiritually, before they were naturally upon the face of the earth. For I, the Lord God, had not caused it to rain upon the face of the earth. For I, the Lord God, had created all the children of men; and not yet a man to till the ground; for in heaven created I them; and there was not yet flesh upon the earth, neither in the water, neither in the air." (Moses 3:5.)

The record gives an interesting account of the creation of Eve as follows:

"And the Lord God caused a deep sleep to fall upon Adam and he slept: and he took one of his ribs, and closed up the flesh instead thereof:

"And the rib, which the Lord God had taken from man, made he a woman, and brought her unto the man.

"And Adam said, This is now bone of my bones, and flesh of my flesh: she shall be called Woman, because she was taken out of man." (Genesis 2:21-23.)

The writer of Proverbs says: "Whoso findeth a wife findeth a good thing, and obtaineth favor with the Lord." (Proverbs 18:22.) Whoso findeth a good husband also findeth a good thing, and whoso findeth some good children findeth some good things. Marriage was intended to be the happiest, healthiest, and most desirable state in all of human existence. God created male and female in the spirit world, and marriage was ordained in heaven before the earth was created. God performed the first marriage before death had entered the world. About marriage, he himself said, "For this cause shall man leave his father and mother, and shall cleave unto his wife. . . . Wherefore they shall be no more twain, but one flesh. What therefore God hath joined together, let not man put asunder." (Matthew 19:4-6.) Thus God established the foundations for the family.

Parents are the source of life, and the family is the sponsoring agency for most of our education, our personal development, our social welfare, our love, our happiness, our character formation, and our religious activities.

169

Even our eternal welfare is based largely on the happiness, love, mutual motivation, and righteousness that are developed in our homes. In no other situation as in marriage has God provided for such joint effort and joint accomplishment. No matter how intelligent or creative one parent may be, he cannot create life by himself, and neither can he establish the solid foundations of character and love by his single effort.

In her sphere the mother has the greatest possible importance. She is the homemaker. She has the strengths of love, faith, and kindness in which she excels. And in many phases of family life she is expected to outperform her husband. Then the family pool their good qualities in a philosophy of all for one and one for all.

The Parent Sins

One of the most common and one of the least understood of all of our activities is that of parenthood. The first requirement of every person is that he must have parents, a father and a mother, and in obedience to the command to multiply and replenish the earth, we have filled the world with offspring.

There are several meanings of the words *father* and *mother*. George Washington was called the father of his country. Gutenberg was the father of printing. The Mississippi River is called the father of waters. Satan was called the father of lies. It has been said that our wishes are the fathers of our thoughts. Our ambitions and our faith are the fathers of our accomplishments.

We speak of the mother church, the mother country, mother earth, the mother spirit, the mother tongue. We speak of the state of Virginia as the mother of presidents because it was the birthplace of eight U.S. presidents— Washington, Jefferson, Madison, Monroe, Harrison, Tyler, Taylor, and Wilson.

Some of the characteristics of all offspring is that they are small and weak when they are born and that the family identities are not always apparent until some later date. Certainly no person or animal ever began life fully grown with the appearance or the power of the parent fully developed. George Washington and Benedict Arnold were both born small and powerless. At first neither of them could walk or talk, and neither of them showed any conclusive evidence of what his final destiny might be. At one time both were great generals, but Washington became the father of his country and Benedict Arnold became its betrayer. While the mothers of Judas Iscariot and Abraham Lincoln were caring for their infant sons, they had no positive idea of how important either of them would become or how far their lives would grow apart.

Just as human beings can be parents, so too are virtues as well as vices capable of parenthood. Bad attitudes and evil deeds may lead to sorrow, loneliness, and misery. As human beings we ought to be mindful of the quality of those parent virtues as well as the parent sins that use us as a matrix for their posterity.

The multiplication of sins in recent years has filled the land with trouble—and they are still breeding and multiplying like compound interest. Suppose we make a list of some of the most dangerous of those deadly parent sins. What would they be? A sampling of them might include such sins as the following:

1. *Bitterness.* We sometimes get into our lives bitter, sour, resentful attitudes that turn us against many of the good things of life. From our bitterness we may hatch out a whole posterity of hate, lust for revenge, or even desire to kill. This is one place where we might

171

very properly use a form of "birth control" to keep bitterness from being born in the first place, so it could never become a parent.

2. *Blaming others.* One important parent sin is that deadly habit of blaming other people for our problems. Fault-finding and the habit of holding grudges can soon fill our systems with deadly poisons. In order to try to keep the infection of these sins cleaned out of our systems, the Lord gave us the powerful law of repentance. He asks us to love our neighbors as ourselves. We should love our enemies and forgive those who trespass against us. The Lord has said that when we undertake to cover up our sins or to gratify our pride or our vain ambition in any degree of unrighteousness, behold, the heavens withdraw themselves, and the Spirit of the Lord is grieved.

3. *Rejection.* It is so easy to develop a destructive antagonism toward someone or something. We oppose religion. We reject God. We fight against righteousness. We even lose our regard for our friends and our families. We sometimes seem to feel a necessity to always prove that we ourselves are right, no matter what the circumstances may be. Then we feel obligated to defend our position. With too much rejection in our hearts we are soon left unto ourselves to kick against the pricks, to persecute others, and to fight against God.

We reject God when we fail to live his commandments, and we reject all good in about that same way. Recently I talked with a couple who had been ideally happy. They had both been good church workers. They were doing well financially and were well mated physically and in personality. Then he let one of these fast-multiplying parent sins get into his life. He began to break that great command of God which says, "Thou shalt love thy wife with all thy heart, and shalt cleave unto her and none else." (D&C 42:22.) He began cleaving to someone else, and when we start compromising with evil, many unpleasant events begin to take place. As he began losing interest in his wife, instead of laying the blame on his infidelity where it belonged, he decided that the reason she had gone down in his affections was because of what she had done. Then he began rationalizing about what a hard life the other woman had had and how she had been mistreated by her former husband, so in order to make up to her for all her troubles, he began displeasing God by his sins and breaking his own wife's heart. He let one problem give birth to a dozen more serious problems.

One man rejected his wife because in having two children she had allowed her weight to go from 106 to 121 pounds. Another rejected his wife because she had muscular dystrophy and he said, "I don't want to be married to a cripple." Those who take one particular marriage vow promise to be true and faithful "for better or for worse, for richer or for poorer, in sickness and in health, until death do us part." Actually, every problem should bring those who love each other closer together rather than allowing the demon of rejection to push them farther apart.

4. *Rebellion.* This is one of the most serious of all of the parent sins. When we rebel against our parents, a lot of disasters befall us. When life seems hard to us, we sometimes fight against God and may even lose our souls. As we rebel against righteousness, we send ourselves to hell. Probably the most serious sins in the world are those of rebellion, with its evil posterity of disloyalty and unfaithfulness.

All sins are destructive to our best interests, but their most dangerous characteristic is that they come linked together in chains and family groups. When we become friendly and invite one evil into our lives, it takes it upon itself to invite all its relatives and associates in. When we destroy one sin, we destroy a multitude that is just waiting to be born. Everyone carries the seeds of many physical diseases in his body, but they do very little damage as long as they are kept inactive. As Goethe said, "I have in me the germ of every crime." But we must not let them start multiplying in us. May the Lord help us to free ourselves from these parent sins and keep our spirits healthy.

Interest

In our language we have an interesting word called *interest*. In one meaning, it represents a share of ownership. The dictionary gives the example of a man who had a one-third interest in a bakery. That meant that he had a one-third right to all of the advantages and profits that came from this business. But this ownership also obligates him to assume one-third of the responsibilities and duties necessary for the bakery's success. We may obtain or lose ownership interests in the greatest things, including happiness and heaven itself. Of one unfortunate soul the Lord said, ". . . he perisheth forever, and hath no interest in the kingdom of God." (Mosiah 4:18.) One of the big questions that will be asked about us when our lives have been finished is, What do our interests consist of?

Interest also means the price or rate paid by a borrower for the use of that which he borrows. When one borrows money he pays a percentage of the principal as rent or interest. Compound interest is when the interest is added to the principal at regular intervals so that we not only get interest on the principal, but also on the interest. Under this program, if we invested $100 at 7 percent interest compounded quarterly, the compound interest would amount to $123,462 in 100 years. Our principal would have been increased over 1200 times.

These sums invested at compound interest work day and night, Sundays and holidays, winter and summer, in all kinds of weather. Compound interest never rests, never takes a vacation, never stops working. It makes a great difference to us whether this power is working for us or against us. Some people never enjoy more than a fraction of the value of their toil because so much of what they earn is eaten up in interest. On the other hand, if interest is working for us, our economic welfare is multiplied. Generally there are two ways to make money. One is by personal labor and the other is to have our money work for us.

I know a man who has had a very intersting life. He has been successful in his business and been active in serving others and trying to make them happy. He has had some beautiful flower gardens and has given the flowers away. He has also helped many people go on missions and has sent others through college. As he has gotten older he has had to cut down on the amount of personal work he does. In order to compensate for this loss in his personal strength and the good that he can do, he has set up a large financial trust made up of the money he has accumulated during his productive years to give him a kind of economic immortality beyond the time of his own death. Through the magic of interest his power to help other people may be continued forever. He has now accumulated enough money to send out after his death more missionaries and to provide more college educations and more flowers to brighten the lives of people than while he was alive. Many of the people he has counseled and helped during his lifetime have already passed away, but he has some wonderful grandchildren and their associates that he would also like to help, and so he has arranged to set up a counseling service for that purpose. The counselors will die and be replaced, but his interest income will guarantee that the service itself will go on.

The word *interest* also indicates a mental state in which we are concerned about something. This is the state in which we are favorably aroused toward some special consideration, when our minds become heated and inflamed with enthusiasm. One great religious leader once said that he was not interested in possessing a religion; he was interested in a religion that would possess him. We may also get so interested in our occupations and our families and our good deeds that, by possessing us, they give us greater power for accomplishment. Victor Hugo once said that there was nothing as powerful as an idea whose time had come. An idea's time always comes as soon as we can harness it and set it to work. An idea's time also arrives when it inspires us and gives a finer incentive for righteous accomplishment.

This kind of driving interest in ideas is more productive than the compound interest paid by financial investments. This kind of interest fosters all of the other kinds. If we have righteous zeal, we can acquire a capital interest in more important things than a bakery. A love of great literature gives us a capital interest in our own culture and refinement. Passion for the holy scriptures gives us a capital investment in the celestial kingdom. The scriptures promise that if we have a sufficient interest in righteousness, we may become celestial beings with a controlling interest in happiness, beauty, love, and all of the other good things represented by heaven itself. How tremendously important is our responsibility to maintain our interest at a high level in the right things! When any wholehearted interest is centered in those hopes or benefits that we desire more ardently for our own lives, miracles can be accomplished.

When Jesus said that we should love God and our neighbors and ourselves and our work, he was saying that we should be intensely interested in them. The scripture says that God is love, and love is a special interest in something that has been fully matured.

The very best way to master any problem is to get interested in it. I know a man who changed his occupation from one he loved but which had limited possibilities to one he disliked but which had unlimited possibilities. This man solved the problem by centering his interest in a job that was productive. He magnified all of its good points and minimized all of its disadvantages. He developed a compelling interest in it. He learned firsthand that if you would like to be successful in something, get intensely interested in it.

Another man has an almost consuming interest in the great literature. In order to capture the exact shade of meaning with all the power that the author intended, he memorizes a large part of it. As he gets older his ability to memorize increases, not that his mind becomes more retentive, but his interest becomes greater.

Recently a middle-aged man announced that he wanted his name taken off the rolls of the Church. In his early life, he had never been very interested in identifying with those great philosophies of life preached by the Master. Church leaders worked with him until a feeble interest had been generated, and for a few years as his interest was pushed by others, he held some responsibilities. But because of his tendency toward evil, his religious interest became too weak to support itself. He deserted his wife and family and stopped going to church. Then he developed bitterness toward the thing he was unrighteously opposing. Because he was violating many of the commandments, he began to fight everything that the Church represented. Naturally, he felt relieved if he could get out of his mind all his ideas of obligations of good so that his conscience would stop bothering him; and he felt that he could do evil to his heart's content if his name was not on the Church records. Therefore, he was excommunicated for apostasy. His evil interests had become strong by exercise.

An important failure factor is called "conflict of interest." We usually screen political candidates very carefully for any interest they have that would tend to destroy the purpose they were elected to serve. Conflicting interests cannot co-exist without damaging each other. They fight each other to a standstill, and they tend to destroy progress on both sides. In life itself a strong enough conflict of interest can make it impossible for us to identify with our finest purposes. Because the motivating powers are lost, success becomes more or less impossible. However, we still allow for too many conflicts of interest to develop in our work and in life itself. Sin can keep us from prayer, and prayer can keep us from sin. A guilty conscience destroys enthusiasm. As a result of his conflict of interest the unprofitable servant said, "I was afraid, and went and hid [my] talent in the ground." (See Matthew 25:25.)

And so we might do well to get a little better acquainted with this excellent and useful word, *interest.* Jesus said that we should lay up treasures in heaven. We can also develop some great treasures in ourselves, such as courage, ambition, enthusiasm, wisdom, and the attitudes and skills of righteousness, which will grow by compound interest to become a mountain of treasure.

Guaranteed
Success

Success might be described as two things: (1) the ability to accept or set for ourselves the proper goals and objectives; (2) the power to bring them about. Someone has said that the first step toward any accomplishment is to believe in it. Our biggest problem is that so many people don't believe in success.

The opposite of success is failure, and while most people give lip service to success, they never seem to get around to making it a part of their own program. We have many ways that we use to actually talk ourselves out of success. We remember Aesop's fable of the fox and the grapes. When the fox failed in his first jump he sealed his failure with an alibi when he said, "The grapes were sour anyway."

Henry Ward Beecher once said that religion had not been tried and found wanting—it had been found hard and not tried. We hear until we are weary about all of the temptations of our day and how difficult it is for us to live our religion. This is merely an excuse, for no temptation is a temptation at all unless we are entertaining it. Every temptation without implies a desire within. Someone has said that we should never say how much the devil tempts, but only how strongly we are inclined. God never forces anyone to do right, and Satan has no power to force us to do wrong.

Jesus said: "Be ye therefore perfect, even as your Father which is in heaven is perfect." (Matthew 5:48.) Another scripture says that God "cannot look upon sin with the least degree of allowance." (D&C 1:31.)

The apostle John says that sin is the transgression of law. That is also a good definition of failure. There are laws of gravity, laws of electricity, and laws of success that never fail unless we transgress them. If we release our hold on a rock, it will fall to the ground; so will a character quality and a standard of values. To reach any success, we need to follow the law. If one wants to be a good cook, he must follow the recipe. If he wants to be a good dressmaker, he must follow the pattern. If he wants to become a good pharmacist, he must follow the prescription. Someone has said that all science is a collection of success formulas.

A famous man was once being interviewed about his success. He said that he had always been successful, even when he was a small boy. He told his questioners that when he and his friends used to hunt birds' eggs, he could always find more eggs than any of the other boys. When they asked for an explanation, he said that he thought it was because he always looked in more bushes. This boy learned one of the laws of success very early in life.

People who become losers are those who do their jobs in the wrong way. Instead of always following the laws of success they merely say, "I'll try it out," or "I'll see how I like it," or "I'll do the best I can." Some try out marriage and attempt to find a life's work that is agreeable to them whether they follow the law or not. Success in marriage isn't just the *big* thing. It is the *only* thing. Marriages fail because someone did something wrong. The greatest marriage partners are those who will not allow the marriage to fail.

If we want to be leaders and guarantee the success of others, we need to develop the good judgment, the generosity, the industry, the spirituality, and the love that go with success. Think of our assignment as parents. What a thrilling experience it is for anyone to be born of goodly parents. With the right kind of parents, it is pretty hard to fail.

We study medicine to learn how to keep ourselves well physically. We study psychology, psychiatry, and other subjects to learn how to keep ourselves well mentally. Agriculture is how we feed ourselves. Sociology is how we live together agreeably. Law is how to keep our lives orderly. Business is how we successfully deal with each other. And we have the gospel and its teachings to learn how to keep ourselves well spiritually.

Religion is how we save our souls and bring about our eternal exaltation. In religion or in life, success is just not the big thing—it is the *only* thing. The one business of life is to succeed. I am sure God did not go to all the trouble of creating this beautiful, wonderful earth without having some wonderful destiny in mind. He did not create us in his own image and endow us with potentially magnificent minds and personalities and surround us with wonders and opportunities, and then expect us to waste our lives in failure. Yet every day many thousands of people fail in the main purposes of their lives.

The Son of God came to earth and established his church among us with the thought in mind that everyone should belong to it. He appointed leaders and instructed them to live so as to be worthy to have his Spirit. He revealed the doctrines of eternal salvation. Then he gave his leaders the authority as well as the command to lead. Good leaders set good examples. They demonstrate a way of life that has been approved by God himself.

On the other hand, how miserable it is to think of leaders who don't lead; of home teachers who don't teach; of the Lord's watchmen who don't watch. All around us there are false friends who consciously or subconsciously are teaching us to depart from morality, religion, and success.

The greatest of our true friends is God, our Eternal Heavenly Father. In the gospel principles he has outlined those things that we must do. If we obey his laws, we may become as he is. God is the only absolutely safe guide in the universe, and we are the ones to put his wisdom in force. If we know him, believe in him, trust him, and obey him, our success is guaranteed. May God bless us to join with him in guaranteeing our eternal success.

The
Corporation

One of the great inventions of our time is the corporation. There are many important things in our world that need to be done, and often there is no one person or group of people who are strong enough, wise enough, or who live long enough to do these things by themselves. There are many workers who need to be trained in skills necessary to enable them to carry forward their part of the work of the world. All of these and many other needs have given rise to the formation of corporations.

However, in the minds of some people there is an actual stigma that attaches to any success, and often criticism is directed toward what we call big business. Yet big business and big science and big government provide the means for us to produce our food, become educated, and raise our standard of living.

A corporation comes into being when a number of people get together and prepare to act as a unit under special rules with some particular purpose in mind. The corporation has its own organization, and the rules regulating its activities must comply with the laws of the land. The corporation is a means of helping us reach our objectives more quickly, effectively, and harmoniously.

A corporation has many abilities that a person or small group of people does not have. It can raise large sums of money to help it accomplish its goals. Through the selling of stock, thousands of others may join with the corporation to assume the risks and share in any profits that may be generated.

Each of us benefits from the activities of large corporations. For example, I have a great experience that comes from my contract with a newspaper corporation, where for a few pennies a newspaper is laid on my front step every day. This is a bargain, because it would be impossible for me as an individual to gather the news throughout the world, write the editorials, collect the accounts of the social happenings, prepare the sports page, get the stock market reports, and draw the comics. In addition, I would have to go to the expense of manufacturing and running the printing presses, building the buildings, growing the paper pulp, and manufacturing the paper. But because of the cooperation of other subscribers, I can have a nicely printed paper delivered to me at a regular time each day for little cost.

Similarly I have at my beck and call the services of hundreds of other corporations. As a customer of an automobile firm, I have the services of scientists studying and working continually to give me the most effective, the nicest-looking automobile fully equipped with radio, temperature controls, lights, power, and speed for my pleasure and profit. Other corporations are similarly working to provide the fuel for my auto.

The airlines have developed other kinds of special equipment for my benefit. They have trained men and women to be pilots, navigators, and stewardesses who are always ready day or night to take me any place on the surface of the earth that I want to go, and they will get me there in the shortest possible time. Many other corporations have been organized to take care of every conceivable need I may have, and they do it in a way that I could not possibly provide for myself at any cost.

Corporations have many other advantages over individuals. They never get sick, and they never die. If one of their scientists or servicemen becomes unable to function effectively, he is replaced by someone else who has already been trained to carry on in my interests.

As a customer I have many safeguards, for corporations are supervised and regulated by appropriate branches of the government. All of them must be competitive with other corporations. If one falls down in its function, it may lose its business to a competitor and the defaulting company may run the risk of going broke. One of the greatest advantages is that the government is merely the referee and not the star performer.

There are some other interesting corporations that are called eleemosynary institutions. These are corporations organized primarily to dispense charity or give away money. Many successful companies and wealthy individuals use their money to establish foundations, the purpose of which is to maintain libraries, operate hospitals, finance colleges, and personally help individuals under certain conditions. The government itself is engaged in an eleemosynary function. It collects taxes from those who are able to pay them and uses the money to reform criminals and give medical care to those who are ill. It also fights delinquency and provides social services for those in need. An immense total of this money goes for direct relief.

When I moved into the city where I now live, the streets were all paved and paid for. The sewer systems had been put in. The power lines had been installed. The stores, churches, and government buildings were in full operation and fully paid for. I may enjoy all of these benefits that have been provided by those who have already passed from this stage of existence.

Of the ten U.S. corporations having the most assets, four are life insurance companies. The greatest values in the world are life values. Because life is very uncertain, any individual person may not live long enough to carry out his ambitions. However, for a set monthly payment, he may buy an insurance policy. Then if his own life is cut short in time, the life insurance company will provide the money to educate his children, pay off the mortgages, give his wife an income to the end of her days, and do other things he might have done had he lived long enough.

Someone has said that a good citizen is one who

puts more back into life than he takes out. He leaves the world better than he finds it. When people produce more than they consume, they leave a surplus that continues to provide eternally such things as libraries, universities, and other benefits that can be had for money. It is a very common practice for corporations and individuals to set up special funds for such purposes.

In similar manner one may provide that when his body is consigned to the grave and his spirit goes back to God who gave it, the wealth that he has set aside may continue to produce an income for carrying on the work of the world and the work of the Lord as though he were actually doing it himself. It is another application of that great passage that says, "Though he were dead, yet shall he live." The most productive of all corporations is the religious corporation. The charter of the church is to teach those life-saving principles of the gospel and minister in all of the necessary ordinances of salvation. It is the job of the church to collect tithing, build churches, erect temples, and send out missionaries. The church's job is to develop faith and cause people to repent of their sins, be baptized, and have hands laid upon them for the gift of the Holy Ghost. Unlike some of the other great corporations, the work of the church is largely done by those who are called into service without remuneration.

In the greatest sermon ever preached, Jesus Christ said that we should lay up for ourselves treasures in heaven. Someone has said about the treasures of the earth that you can't take them with you. That may not be entirely accurate. The thing that we spend more time doing than anything else is in our employment; and those treasures of the earth that may come as a consequence may be translated into character, temple work, missionary work, and all sorts of other things that can be taken with us. In addition, that accumulation which is left behind may continue forever to store up additional treasures in heaven. Even after our death we may continue to assist God to bring to pass the immortality and eternal life of man.

Each one of us has a kind of corporation soul in his own life, and may God help us to operate it with constant wisdom.

Saltwater Remedies

Some time ago I heard a prominent educator declare that the reason we don't get better solutions for our problems is that we try to cure our difficulties by indulging in too many of the wrong kinds of solutions. This educator referred to these solutions as "saltwater remedies." For example, if your problem was that you had an extreme thirst and someone offered you a sparkling glass of saltwater, your thirst would only be made greater. This was the educator's idea of a saltwater remedy.

We should not try to cure our problems with remedies that don't remedy, but only make our situation worse. Salt has a chemical property that attracts and holds water, and if you take in more salt, it attracts the moisture that you already have in your system and prevents it from doing its assigned job. In other words, additional salt causes you to have greater thirst rather than relieves that which you already have.

We remember Samuel Coleridge's story of the ancient mariner whose ship was becalmed on an ocean. Because no rains fell, the sailors had no fresh water. The ancient mariner said, "Water, water, everywhere, nor any drop to drink." Finally, one by one, his sailors died of thirst.

Salt is a common substance in nature, and in small quantities we use it to season our food. It is used as a preservative. It has an ability to change temperatures. We use it to melt snow on our streets in winter. We sometimes use it as a gargle to kill disease. But one of its properties is certainly not that of quenching thirst.

The Dead Sea is 26 percent salt, and at the southern end of the sea is a mountain of salt measuring seven miles long and several hundred feet high. The Great Salt Lake also has a high concentration of salt, and volumes of salt deposits many feet thick make up the floor of what used to be the old Lake Bonneville.

We sometimes have in our lives troubles that may be compared to these vast deposits of salt, and one of our biggest difficulties arises because so frequently we try to cure these problems by applying saltwater remedies. For example, I know a man who has always seemed to be a little short on cash, and in trying to solve this problem, he has attempted to get the additional money he needs by doing some forging. He has just been released after serving four and a half years in the state penitentiary. In order to provide himself with an additional $200, he lost a good job with a very promising future. He lost four and a half years of pay and a good reputation. This man's attempt to solve his financial problems not only solved none of his problems, but created many new ones.

Some time ago a man was telling me of his drinking problem. He had undergone a long struggle to cure himself of his thirst for liquor. With the help of friends and Alcoholics Anonymous he thought he had gotten the poison completely out of his system, and then on one occasion he joined a group of friends engaged in some social drinking. Again he felt the thirst for a drink, and he thought that just one little friendly drink wouldn't hurt him. He took the saltwater remedy of drinking liquor, and now he is back into more trouble than he was to begin with.

Recently a young woman came to talk about some of

her problems. By nature she was a loving, warm-hearted person who liked gaiety and company. But in trying to solve some of her problems she got mixed up with the wrong kind of people, and through their influence she got a lot of evil into her life. She was trying to cure her need for company by saltwater methods. She discovered to her sorrow that improper relations with immoral friends did not satisfy her desire for the feeling of security and companionship, but instead made her social and moral problems much worse. Now she is hooked on some bad habits and a bad reputation that make her goals in life more difficult than they were before.

Someone has said, "You can lead a horse to water but you cannot make him drink." However, there are ways to make the horse thirsty and then he will drink by himself. All you need to do is to put a little salt in his oats or on his hay and you will be unable to keep him away from the water. And if he drinks pure, clear water he can solve his problem. But if you also put a lot of salt in the watering trough, the horse may soon be dead of thirst. A similar situation applies to us. Satan has no power to force us to do wrong, but he can still accomplish his purpose when he makes the salt of evil easily available to us, and then we tend to destroy ourselves by his poisonous remedies.

We hear till we are weary about the temptations of our day. Temptations beset us on every hand. They are in the movies and the magazines. It sometimes seems that almost everything we see or hear or read has some temptation in it drawing us downward. However, the problem is not in the temptation, but in our attitude toward it. No temptation is a temptation at all unless we are entertaining it. We blame Satan for a lot of our problems where we should pile the blame on our own unwise attempts to solve our problems by improper means. It is by overcoming problems that we develop ourselves.

Someone has said: "We pray for strength and God gives us difficulties to overcome. We ask for wisdom and God sends us problems, the solution of which develops wisdom. We pray for ability and God gives us a brain and brawn with which to work."

If we want to develop strong muscles, we get a heavy job to do. God always fits the back to the burden, and we can solve almost any problem when we have good judgment, right decisions, industry, and high standards of righteousness. Someone once said to President Abraham Lincoln that his eyes looked tired and they thought he should rest. President Lincoln said, "It is my heart that is tired, and in order to rest my heart, I have to go on at an accelerated pace." If you have a son who is tired of school, the best way to cure his problem is not for him to quit school to rest up. That is a saltwater remedy. The way to solve his problem is for him to work twice as hard at his studies and get ahead in his work. No one ever gets bored while he is winning. Usually we do not get tired while we are ahead. The pace that kills is the crawl. We can sleep better at night if we work harder during the daytime. As we keep ourselves physically healthy with pure water, good food, and plenty of exercise, so we keep ourselves spiritually strong and mentally stable with righteous conduct and good attitudes. When we try to make ourselves happy by indulging bad habits or exercising negative attitudes, we are drinking the saltwater that will make them worse and may finally even destroy our souls.

There are some people, who, when they want to have fun, go out and get drunk, but this is a saltwater prescription. Drunkards are never really happy. Criminals are not happy. Immoral people are the most miserable people in the world because they destroy their peace of mind by indulging their saltwater remedies in attempting to appease their appetites. All evil practices are saltwater remedies.

We lose much of the great power God has invested in the human personality and fail to develop the great spirituality he intended us to have because of too many saltwater remedies. Just think how many things we do that actually increase our problems rather than offer us any cure.

We go through life bothered by our fears and our feelings of guilt instead of correcting them with superior behavior and righteousness. Many people complain of loneliness in their lives, but there are also a lot of good ways to overcome loneliness. When we keep ourselves busy doing friendly, interesting, constructive things for others, life always takes on more interest. On the other hand, we can increase our loneliness by those saltwater remedies of magnifying our troubles, being pessimistic, and feeling sorry for ourselves.

All of us have needs that must be satisfied. We can't go without food for more than about thirty days; we can't go without water for more than about three days; we can't go without air for more than about three minutes; and we can't go without a good opinion of ourselves for very long without getting our lives all mixed up. We need self-confidence and interest in life to make our lives happy. The one burden that is too heavy for anyone to bear is to feel that his own life is not worthwhile.

Jesus said, ". . . blessed are all they that do hunger and thirst after righteousness; for they shall be filled with the Holy Ghost." (Matthew 5:6, Inspired Version.) He said to the woman of Samaria, "Whosoever drinketh of this water shall thirst again; But whosoever drinketh of the water that I shall give him shall never thirst; but the water that I shall give him shall be in him a well of water springing up into everlasting life." (John 4:13-14.) This water will wash out the impurities and make our lives wholesome and strong.

The Lord has given us another purifier in the

190

principle of repentance. Because we cannot make a right with two wrongs, whenever we get an evil into our hearts, instead of trying for a cure by taking in other poisons, we should wash out the one that is already there with repentance and righteousness. Otherwise, we magnify our problems rather than eliminate them.

A roadside billboard of an oil company says, "A clean engine produces power," and so does a clean mind and a clean heart. May the Lord help us to keep out of our lives those saltwater remedies that make life unsuccessful.

Mud

Recently a good friend of mine was trying to identify some word in our language that would be the least meaningful and have the minimum amount of significance and prestige. She finally settled on the little three-letter word M-U-D.

The dictionary says that mud is a sticky, slippery substance formed by mixing water with dirt. Mud also serves as a symbol for belittlement. When we want to deflate someone or something, we may refer to them or to it as mud or dirt. We describe the lowest kind of behavior as dirty. Probably the worst anyone can say about any of the forms of dirt itself is to call it by its own name, DIRT, for there is no word insignificant enough to belittle dirt. In its dry state, dirt becomes dust, which can be very unpleasant to deal with. Even when a good rain solves the problems of dust, it may cause an equal difficulty by creating a sea of sticky, slippery mud.

One of the favorite scenes in the old Mack Sennett comedies was to see someone dressed in his best clothes fall on his face in the mud. Even since the days of Mack

Sennett, in one way or another, people continue to fall into a lot of different kinds of mud puddles, both symbolic and otherwise. In fact, the number one problem of our day is dirt: dirty government, dirty business, dirty people, and dirty attitudes. We have far too much mud-slinging in our politics, but we have even more in our marriages. Muddy roads and muddy fields will dry up in time, but muddy thinking, muddy outlooks on life, and muddy morals seem to get continually worse. One of our greatest needs is to get ourselves out of the mud. And we might keep in mind that no one ever fell into any kind of a mud who didn't first get too close to it.

On the other hand, there are many things about mud that we should be grateful for. One is that God put all dirt under our feet and a clean, life-giving atmosphere over our heads. What might life be like if he had reversed this order? Dirt also has a clean side; it is probably nature's greatest purifier. All kinds of human, animal, and plant waste and filth returned to the earth become fertilizer. Even worn-out and diseased plants and animals can be used by the earth to enrich itself. This combination of dirt + water = mud is undoubtedly a great asset. This is especially true because of its close alliance with the warm, life-saving rays from the sun.

God made a great contribution to us when he covered our earth with a wonderful layer of topsoil. This thin layer of dirt has in it millions of times more value than all of the minerals, metals, oil, and precious gems put together. When we use up our mineral resources they are gone forever, but dirt is everlasting and productive. The soil is like a miraculous bank account from which we can endlessly draw many substances without decreasing the original in the slightest. Supported by a cultivator and a little fertilizer, with assistance from the sun, the air, and the rain, topsoil becomes a marvelous manufacturing plant turning out the choicest vegetables, the most nutritious grains, the most delicious fruits, and the finest meat.

Recently I was trying to help a man and his wife solve some of their marital problems. One of his points of contention was that she had referred to him as dirt. In trying to help heal his wounds, I said, "I can prove that she is absolutely right." Then I read to him from the account of creation wherein it was said, "Thus the heavens and the earth were finished. . . . but the Lord God had not caused it to rain upon the earth, and there was not a man to till the ground." (Genesis 2:1, 5.) And then, I suppose, so that it would stick together, the Creator added a little water to his dust. At least the record says: "But there went up a mist from the earth, and watered the whole face of the ground. And the Lord God formed man of the dust of the ground, and breathed into his nostrils the breath of life; and man became a living soul." (Genesis 2:6-7.)

The first question Adam and Eve were asked to decide was whether or not they would eat the fruit from the tree of knowledge of good and evil, which came out of the ground. After they had eaten, God said: "Behold, the man is become as one of us, to know good and evil. . . ." (Genesis 3:22.) I would just like to point out in passing that the right kind of knowledge still tends to have that effect upon people. To eat of the fruit from the tree of knowledge still tends to make men and women become as God. And what is even more exciting is to contemplate God's promise that if we are faithful, he will someday invite us to eat the fruit from the tree of life.

Many years ago I sat before a sculptor who had been engaged by a university to sculpt a bust in bronze. As he was finishing the clay model, he invited my wife and me to come to his studio to see his nearly finished work, and while we were there he would put on the finishing touches. We took our young daughter with us. While we spent some time discussing other matters with the sculptor, our daughter began browsing around the studio. Suddenly she was startled by unexpectedly coming upon this nearly finished clay model. With great excitement she shouted, "Daddy! Daddy! Come here quick! There is a piece of mud over here that looks exactly like you!" And so it did. And if anyone refers to me as dirt, he will be technically correct. God formed Adam out of the dust of the earth, which had first been watered by the mist. And, according to the dictionary definition, this would make us all some variety of mud.

Each of us also helps to create himself out of the dust by what he eats and drinks. Our food comes out of the topsoil and, in addition, chemists have estimated that we are all 70 percent water. It might even help us to have better attitudes toward ourselves if we realized that in addition to those elements, there has also been mixed into us a little of that wonderful sunshine that comes down upon our heads. We ourselves are the finest products of the earth.

We can increase the values of our lives by attracting the more godly elements. It bothers me to hear the evolutionists expound their theories that man evolved from some low, one-celled form of life. There is the far more wonderful explanation. The scripture says, ". . . there is a spirit in man: and the inspiration of the Almighty giveth it understanding." (Job 32:8.)

I am sure that God did not go to all of the trouble of creating this wonderful earth without having a grand destiny in mind for those whom he permitted to live here upon it. John L. McCreary expressed something of the miracle that comes from the earth when he said:

The dust we tread beneath our feet
Shall change beneath the summer showers
To golden grain and mellow fruit
And rainbow-tinted flowers.

The granite rocks disorganize
To feed the hungry moss they bear;
The forest-leaves drink daily life
From out the viewless air.

We may attract from life the most inspiring elements. In every choice in life we have at least two points of view to select from. Someone has said, "Two men look out through iron bars. One sees the mud, the other sees the stars." Every condition of our lives will be placed on more solid ground if we always look at the perfection that is inherent in our earthly possibilities.

Jesus announced our most noble concept, indicating our highest destiny, when he quoted an ancient scripture in which God says, "Ye are gods; and all of you are children of the most High." (Psalm 82:6.) God's law of heredity indicates that if we are faithful, we may someday become like our eternal parents. And if, along the way, someone should sometime call us "a stick-in-the-mud," that might make us all the more grateful for our final godly destiny. As we stand with our feet on the earth, may God help us to keep our eyes on the stars.

A Success Kit

We have some interesting words in our language that are important to the success of what we do. One of these is the word *kit*. The dictionary says that a kit is a set of implements used in an occupation. It is a collection of necessary personal effects that form a part of one's equipment. There are also kits that help us live life more effectively. Poet R. L. Sharpe refers to this situation when he says:

195

To each is given a bag of tools,
A shapeless mass and a book of rules;
And each must make, ere life is flown,
A stumblingblock or a steppingstone.

Man himself is a great success kit. The scriptures call people by different titles. The Lord said to Ezekiel: "Son of man, I have made thee a watchman unto the house of Israel." (Ezekiel 3:17.) Solomon said: "The spirit of man is the candle of the Lord." (Proverbs 20:27.) In the scriptures certain men are called by such titles as prophets, messengers, ministering spirits, apostles, and missionaries.

Suppose we try to analyze ourselves and identify those important tools used by us to bring about our own success. We will find that they are mostly a part of ourselves. The apostle Paul, in his famous twelfth chapter of First Corinthians, compared the spiritual gifts as well as the officers of the church to the human body and said that all were necessary; that the hand could not say to the foot, "I have no need of thee." Man, the greatest creation of God, has no parts that are superfluous or useless. In a very important way a human being can be compared to a kit of tools, every member of which is important and serves some useful function.

God fashioned each part of us to aid in bringing about some particular success. He has given us brains with which to think and plan and organize our work. A human brain is about the size of one's two hands and is made up of fourteen billion cells. It is the greatest creation of God himself; there is nothing like it in the universe. With it we have the power to set objectives, build character, and make resolutions.

As a part of our success kit each of us has been given a personality. None other of God's creations can even smile, and our personalities make God our only fellow in the universe. A survey some time ago indicated that most of the things that we do that result in failure or success are not because of mere competence or incompetence. Our failures come about because of personality traits. We may be negative or positive, pleasant or unpleasant, weak or strong. We may be a failure or a success, or good or bad, according to our own choices.

It is interesting that God has given his human creations these gifts that are so far above the other works of his hands. He tied the trees and other vegetation to the earth so that they could not move about in any attempt to improve their own situation. Animals were given the privilege of movement but they are limited in what they do by a set of instincts they can do nothing about. In addition, they are unable to learn any new thing. But men and women are permitted to move over the earth in any direction at any time when they think it would give them any advantage or satisfaction.

No generation of animals has ever learned anything from any previous generation; they all respond according to the specifications that were put into creation's package thousands of years ago. That is, roosters crow in the same key today as they did in the days of Nebuchadnezzar, king of Babylonia. Bees store their honey in the same size of hexagonal cell as they did thousands of years ago in ancient Egypt. There is very little difference in their behavior or needs, and they have limited personal equipment to work with.

No horse can ever learn to use a saw or a hammer or a pair of pliers. Not even the most intelligent horse can learn to open a gate or turn on a water tap or build himself a shelter from the cold or even shake hands with another horse. A horse has legs that are stronger than man's and yet no horse can climb a ladder, do a tap dance, or put on ice skates. No animal ever learns to read or to memorize the holy scriptures. Animals know nothing at all about God, their Creator, or what their final destiny is to be. No animal is ever thrilled by musical concerts or scientific lectures. It seems that the animals were created not to serve themselves, but to serve us. Horses work, cows give milk, chickens lay eggs, and pigs manufacture bacon, whereas people laugh, love, converse, work, and sing. The Lord said, "Man is, that he might have joy." (2 Nephi 2:25.) Man's primary purpose is to build up his own happiness, and every part of man was created as an instrument of his success.

Men were put together mysteriously by their Creator. David has said that we are fearfully and wonderfully made, and we were built for an eternity of progress and increase. (See Psalm 139:14.) Just think of the great value of the human gift of language. How tragic it is when we let our kit of tools go rusty because they are not used. Someone has made a list of ten great human sins that we commit against ourselves, which we express by saying:

1. I didn't think.
2. I don't believe.
3. I don't understand.
4. I don't care.
5. I am too busy.
6. I don't know.
7. I am too tired.
8. I leave well enough alone.
9. I don't have time to read.
10. I am not interested.

And so we come back to the fundamental proposition that we each have a miraculous kit within ourselves, the ultimate purpose of which is to make us become even as God. May God help us to learn to use all of our equipment for its highest purpose.

He That Hath Eyes,
Let Him See

Of all of the miracles and wonders I have heard about, nothing surpasses the miracle of eyesight, which beholds the glory of the sun, can reach out across the universe to the most distant star, and can bring back to us all the beauties and wonders of the world.

Jesus pointed out that some of us have eyes that don't see and ears that don't hear and hearts that fail to understand. Because these gifts are granted us only on a kind of lend-lease basis, when we fail to use them, they lose their potentiality and consequently our lives themselves are let down from the high place that the Lord intended them to occupy. These gifts are also sometimes taken from us by processes of aging or ill health.

After I had had nearly seventy years of abundant good health the optometrist discovered in my eyes the seeds of retinal deterioration that would eventually rob me of my ability to read. It is a situation in which the central vision of the eye loses its ability to function. For several years I have suffered the effects of this downward trend in my physical vision. One by one some of the pleasures of reading, the joy of seeing clearly the expressions on the faces of my friends, and the light in the eyes of my grandchildren have been gradually taken away. Consequently, my life has become more solitary than before. I frequently become lonesome for the faces of my friends and for the pleasant association formerly had with friends living in the pages of great literature. Much of my association has been cut off with some of the ancient and modern prophets. And because I can no longer read newspaper print, I miss keeping up-to-date on the happenings of our own age of miracles and wonders.

When the apostle Paul was imprisoned in his Roman dungeon to await his execution, he wrote a letter to Timothy, asking him to bring Paul's coat to the prison to keep him warm through the long cold months of the approaching winter and also to bring him his books. Paul reminded Timothy that he was particularly anxious to have him bring his beloved parchments. I'm sure that Paul felt if he had his coat to keep him warm and his books to keep his mind profitably employed, he would get through the winter all right. And what a great joy it would be to me if for an hour or two a day I could borrow a couple of good retinas while I fed on some of the great philosophies, the wonderful poems, and the great scriptures of those enchanting books that have lost some of their ability to lift me up, though they still occupy their accustomed places on my bookshelves.

I have no serious feelings of guilt or regret because of my present inability to read, for I have read a great deal and have enjoyed it very much. I have memorized many stimulating passages. But I miss the ability not only to explore, but to reread. We usually like those things best that we are most familiar with. We like to sing the familiar songs. Children like to hear the same story over and over again. We love to read the biographies of the people we know. We love the great literature that is most familiar to us.

Shakespeare wrote thirty-seven plays and staffed them with 1,000 characters, each of whom is the personification of some personality trait. Some of these children of Shakespeare's creative imagination are among my finest friends. I love to go into the courtroom at Venice and hear Portia make her plea to Shylock for mercy for the unfortunate Antonio, or hear her inspiring expression of love to her betrothed husband, Lord Bessanio. I love to listen to Henry V give his impassioned speech of arousal to his soldiers before the battle of Agincort, or to hear Julius Caesar give his philosophies of courage. Caesar said: "Cowards die many times before their deaths;/The valiant never taste of death but once./Of all the wonders that I yet have heard,/It seems to me most strange that men should fear;/Seeing that death, a necessary end,/Will come when it will come."

I like to walk through the pages of *Paradise Lost* with John Milton. I have a particular interest in Milton, because he was blind for some twenty years before *Paradise Lost* was written. Someone has said that John Milton never saw paradise until he lost his eyes. He said of his own blindness:

Seasons return; but not to me returns
Day, or the sweet approach of ev'n or morn,
Or sight of vernal bloom, or summer's rose,
Or flocks, or herds, or human face divine;
But cloud instead, and ever-during dark
Surrounds me, from the cheerful ways of men
Cut off, and for the book of knowledge fair
Presented with a universal blank,
Of Nature's works, to me expung'd and raz'd,
And wisdom at one entrance quite shut out.

John Milton's first wife died, and he married again after he was blind. He often wondered what she looked like and wished that he could see her, but he was blind. Then one night he saw her in his dream. He thought he had never imagined anything quite so beautiful. He said: "Vested all in white, pure as her mind, love's goodness, sweetness in her person shined so clear that nothing could have rendered more delight. But, oh, as to embrace me she inclined, I waked, she fled and day brought back my night."

When John Milton was awake, he was blind. Only in the nighttime did he have eyes. Contemplating this loss, he said, "Light, the prime work of God in me extinct, with all her various wonders of delight." He prayed that inasmuch as physical light had been denied him, God would grant him the gift of spiritual vision so he might see and understand the things of God. Then in concluding his prayer, he said: "So much the rather thou celestial light shine inward and the mind with all her powers irradiate. There plant eyes, all mists from hence purge and disperse, that I may see and tell of things invisible to mortal sight."

I have another special interest in the blind Greek poet Homer, who lived nine centuries B.C. He wrote the great epic poems, *The Iliad* and *The Odyssey*. *The Iliad* is a story of the valor and heroism displayed in the ten-year Trojan War, and *The Odyssey* is the account of the Greek hero Odysseus and his ten-year adventurous return trip from the battlefields of Troy back to his Greek kingdom, Ithaca. I love to read the potent passages of these experiences because I feel a relationship and an intimacy with those who take part.

And most exciting of all, I like to devour the holy scriptures and live with the prophets and hear the word of God himself. I can stand at the foot of Mount Sinai and, to the accompaniment of the lightnings and thunders of that sacred mountain, hear the divine voice giving those laws called the Ten Commandments. In imagination I can go to the top of the Mount of Transfiguration and see Jesus transfigured before Peter, James, and John. I may stand at the foot of the cross as the Son of God made the sacrifice by which he redeemed all of mankind, including me, and made eternal exaltation possible on condition of our own good works.

Sometimes our senses deteriorate with age or lose their power because of disuse, sin, or perverted interests. And so I would say with Jesus, "Having eyes, see ye not? and having ears, hear ye not?" (Mark 8:18.) While we have minds and hearts capable of under-standing, we ought to use them to the limit.

How grateful I am that though some things have been taken, yet many still abide. I can still hear the testimonies of my friends and feel their enthusiasm. I have an increase of gratitude for those other gifts of God of which I have a full use.

My earnest prayer to my Heavenly Father is that my ears may hear and my heart may clearly understand those important truths that are so necessary to our eternal success and happiness.

The
Golden Age

Since time began, people have had an intense attraction to the metallic substance that we call gold. Gold is one of the most precious of our metals. It has been used through many centuries as a valuable medium of exchange. It is an excellent bartering agent by which we may obtain other things. We may count our wealth in terms of its equivalent in gold. Gold is more malleable than most other metals and can be easily fashioned into beautiful jewelry and other ornaments. It has a higher specific density than most other materials. One cubic foot of gold weighs 1,210 pounds; one and three-quarters cubic feet of gold weighs over a ton. A cubic foot of gold would weigh nineteen times as much as a cubic foot of water.

Many parts of Solomon's temple were overlaid with pure gold. When the temple in Jerusalem was destroyed by Nebuchadnezzar, vessels of gold were taken to Babylon to serve in the palace of the king. (Daniel 5:3.) We sometimes hear of the streets of heaven as being paved with gold. In his revelation concerning our earth's future existence, John saw the New Jerusalem when it shall descend out of heaven after the second coming of Christ, and he said, ". . . and the city was pure gold, like unto clear glass. . . . and the street of the city was pure gold, as it were transparent glass." (Revelation 21:18, 21.)

A beautiful story is told about a house with golden windows. Jesus gave us a superb rule of conduct called the Golden Rule. Up until 1935, in our financial affairs we had a gold standard of measurement for all of our money. In marriage we also have the custom of observing a golden wedding anniversary.

We have a term, "fine gold," for gold that has a highly pure content. We make a similar application to people by saying they are fine people, pure gold.

Over the centuries, periods of great prosperity and progress have been referred to as golden ages. This designation was used by the Greek poet Homer to describe a period of the past that he considered more civilized and enlightened than his own. Homer had no written records that described such a period, but he might have been acquainted with the traditions of the famous Mycenaean and Cretan civilizations that had flourished long before his time.

Historians have applied the phrase "golden age" to a period when a nation reaches its highest peak of achievement, particularly in the arts, literature, sciences, and philosophy. For example, historians maintain that the golden age of Greece actually dawned in the age of Pericles, from 461 to 431 B.C., long after Homer's time. During that period, Athens reached great heights in sculpture, architecture, and drama.

Aristotle mentions four cardinal virtues that helped the Greeks achieve their high place: courage, temperance, justice, and wisdom. Plato defined courage as endurance of the soul, justice as excellence of the soul, temperance as health of the soul, and wisdom as communion of the soul with reality.

The Greeks did not find virtue easy. Aristotle said,

"Excellence is much labored for by the race of men," and the Greek poet Hesiod said, "Before the gates of excellence, the high gods have placed sweat; long is the road thereto, and steep, and rough."

Socrates went around Athens trying to develop the wisdom of his fellow Athenians so they could understand truth. He was wise enough to know that no man could see the truth about other things unless he first saw the truth about himself, and to show a man the truth about himself isn't exactly a popular procedure.

Plato pointed out that there exists in every man a spark of good that must be developed. This is the spark that John called the light that "lighteth every man that cometh into the world" (John 1:9), light that exists in every human being and that can be kindled into a bright flame to lighten the whole world. However, Alfred the Great pointed out that "power is never good, except he be good that has it." × × ×

If we could effectively follow these wise and important principles we might all reach a golden age.

Many other nations have also enjoyed eras described as their golden age. Historians would probably agree on the following:

Egypt, the golden age of literature, 2200-2050 B.C.; the golden age of wealth and empire, 1500-1385 B.C.

Rome, 27 B.C.-A.D. 14, the age of Augustus.

Mexico, 1440-1520, the reign of the Montezumas.

Spain, 1474-1516, the reign of Ferdinand V and Isabella I.

England, 1558-1603, the reign of Elizabeth I.

France, 1640-1740, the reigns of Louis XIV and Louis XV.

People often regard the legendary past of their ancestors as their golden age of glory. They usually have few facts, but use their imaginations to fill the times with the highest virtues and ideals. They speak of the "good old days" as having been the best.

205

All of these are relatively unimportant when compared with the golden possibilities each one of us has.

For the most wonderful period in history, we should not look only back into the past. Branch Rickey, the famous baseball manager, when asked to describe his finest day in baseball, said, "I can't, because I haven't had it yet." Certainly we should do those things that enable us to look ahead and not back for our most exciting period of life both as individuals and as civilizations.

A golden age is brought about not by golden sunsets or golden windows or golden goblets; it is brought about by golden people. A great admiral once said that he would rather have "iron men in wooden boats than wooden men in iron boats." We are better off as golden men in a corrupt age than as corrupt men in a golden age. The aim of wisdom is to develop golden men with a golden touch to live in a golden age. A great society can only be brought about by golden men with golden philosophies. The golden age of Greece would not have been what it was without Pericles, Socrates, Sophocles, Demosthenes, Euripedes, and Aristotle. The age was made great because of the accomplishments of its artists and sculptors, philosophers, and statesmen.

The Bible points us forward to a time when we may live in a golden city upon this earth. This shall come about after the cleansing of the corruption that is presently destroying our atmosphere. What a great era of prosperity we might expect during the millennial reign of Christ, when the evil that presently holds us back shall be eliminated, permitting people to go forward to unheard-of prosperity and progress. Then we may have a golden age of morality, a golden age of enjoyment, a golden age of accomplishment.

We might think of the golden age of America as that time when the people gained their freedom. The United States was established with a divine constitution that

God himself had provided for by raising up wise men for that very purpose. What tremendous opportunities we have to establish in the world a new golden age of wisdom, of reason, of godliness. Our forefathers lived on a flat, stationary earth and plowed their ground with a wooden stick, while we live on an earth of power steering and jet propulsion. But we need the character and personality qualities to match our opportunities. We have a golden age made up by men of tin.

In many ways ours is the most progressive age. Some time ago, it was reported that 80 percent of all the scientists who have ever lived upon the earth are alive today. We are making greater progress in many areas than has ever been known before in the world, but we are also being held back because we are mixing too much of the dross of corruption into the gold of progress. Some of that which dazzles our eyes is merely fool's gold, and it would certainly be ridiculous to build a golden age for fools.

God did not reserve his greatest scientists, his greatest professional men, his greatest captains of industry to come to earth in this dispensation of the fulness of times without also reserving for this period his greatest prophets, his wisest teachers, and those having the finest character qualities. The greatest golden age that can be built must follow the directions of Deity, and God has indicated that it can only be established upon a foundation of genuine wisdom.

At the time the earth is cleansed of its sins, those ripened in foolishness will be destroyed, and Christ, the God of wisdom, will reign for a thousand years. After the millennium, the celestial kingdom of God will be established upon this earth. If we want to be golden people then, we should begin by being golden people now.

For thousands of years alchemists have tried to transmute the baser metals, such as iron and lead, into gold, and they have not yet been successful. The only way to bring about a golden age is through golden people. Each of us has that individual power of a golden touch within himself. We don't need to wait a thousand years or even for one more minute. We may be golden parents, golden children, golden citizens today. We can make golden lives by building our lives on the rocks of wisdom and excellence. What could give us a greater thrill or incentive for accomplishment than to renew in our lives the attraction for pure gold and to strengthen our abilities to get this valuable element in operation in our own personal lives!

The United Order

The scriptures speak about an interesting religious practice that has sometimes been used over the ages to promote the economic welfare of people. This program has been known by various names, such as the United Order, the Order of Enoch, the Law of Consecration. It is based on the philosophy of an ideal economic order in which everyone works to the full limit of his ability, and each member has the privilege of withdrawing from the total accumulation according to his need rather than according to his ability to contribute. In the ideal operation of this program, no one has that which is above another, and those who are sick or have large families or other kinds of problems share in the total—not according to any equity, but according to what their needs may be.

We hear of this unique arrangement first in the days of Enoch, one of the greatest prophets who ever lived on this earth. Enoch was ordained to the priesthood at age

25. At age 65 he was set apart by Adam to go on a mission to teach righteousness among the wicked, and for the next 365 years he worked continuously at his call. He gathered his people together in the city of Enoch, about which the scripture says: "And the Lord called his people Zion, because they were of one heart and one mind, and dwelt in righteousness; and there was no poor among them." (Moses 7:18.)

We might try to imagine a society in which there were no poor, no slums, no idlers, and no sinners. Apparently this idea worked pretty well in the entire city of Enoch, for all its people were eventually translated and taken up into heaven.

This economic order was also practiced for a time in the days of Jesus. In Acts 2:44 we find this reference: "And all that believed were together, and had all things common." The scripture also says: "And the multitude of them that believed were of one heart and of one soul: neither said any of them that ought of the things which he possessed was his own, but they had all things common." (Acts 4:32.)

There was also a period of great righteousness among the Nephites. Of them the record says: "And they had all things common among them; therefore there were not rich and poor, bond and free, but they were all made free, and partakers of the heavenly gift." (4 Nephi 3.)

This program would mean a utopia among us if we had the righteousness and self-control to make it work. We can understand some of the advantages of this kind of arrangement to help solve the inequities among us. One father may have ten children to support and another may have no dependents at all, or there may be much more sickness and fewer opportunities in one family than in another, and these inequities cut down the financial privileges of such people. But because of human weaknesses, this system has never seemed to work very well for very long. We have too much selfishness and too many idlers to make any common program work very well. There are too many people who want to take more out of life than they put in.

To make this higher law really work, everyone would need to be ambitious, virtuous, and love his neighbor as himself. It would be necessary for each one to live as near to the top of his condition as possible. Because we haven't been able to qualify for the United Order, the Lord has instituted some lesser laws, including tithing, fast offerings, and other welfare programs. However, because of our personal weaknesses and lack of faith, even these lesser laws are not obeyed very well.

The United Order idea has other interesting possibilities. We do have access to the sunshine and the atmosphere in common. The beauty of the entire earth is ours to behold and enjoy. Someone has said, "I own the landscape." For all practical purposes, we also own the mountains and the oceans, the moon, and even the sun.

We have the scriptures in common. Those who are poor and those who are rich, if they are worthy, may share equally in the use of the temples. The scriptures say that everyone will be judged according to his works, and if we properly prepare ourselves, each may labor in the work of the Lord to his heart's content. Our access to God and the celestial kingdom is had by us in common with the most wealthy.

Emerson has said that we live in the lap of an immense intelligence and we may draw therefrom according to our own needs and desires. The most favored among us are not always born in the palaces of princes, and frequently over the head of genius we find a roof of straw.

Shakespeare said: "Assume a virtue if you have it not." There are no copyrights or patents on virtues, ambitions, or abilities. All good characters and personality traits may be had in common if we will only take the time to develop them.

When we put our knowledge of medicine on a kind of United Order basis, every doctor and everyone else in the world is entitled to take advantage of the newest methods, ideas, and discoveries with little or no charge. I have just finished reading a book written by the man who, so far as I know, is the greatest salesman in the world. He has developed within himself information and techniques that enable him to be more prosperous and more successful in his field than anyone else on earth. This same information is available to everyone on a United Order basis. That is, this man has not only written all of this information down for others to apply, but he is willing to tell his associates, competitors, friends, and enemies every detail of his success secrets. It wouldn't be considered very good form to pick this man's pockets and take away that money which he has already earned. However, he gives everyone the unlimited and more valuable privilege of picking his brains and his spirit, so they may acquire from him the source of supply rather than merely the result.

Certainly this concept of a United Order is one of the most valuable ideas that our world has produced. The only problem involved is that so frequently we fail to take advantage of these opportunities.

Many years ago Joseph Addison wrote an interesting parable titled "A Mountain of Miseries." He had been pondering over the celebrated thought of Socrates that "if the misfortunes of mankind were cast into a common stock and then equally distributed to everyone of those who now think themselves the most unfortunate, they would be even more miserable with their new allotment of troubles." Socrates contended that the hardships and misfortunes that so concern us now would be far more agreeable than those we would get if we traded with any other person.

211

Mr. Addison says that as he was turning this idea over in his mind, he fell asleep and dreamed that Jupiter issued a proclamation that every mortal should bring his griefs and calamities to an area appointed for this purpose and throw them down together in a common pile. In his dream Mr. Addison was stationed in the center of the area, where he could observe everything that took place. His heart was melted as one by one he saw the whole human species marching by groaning and moaning under their burdens of grief and miseries; then, in obedience to the decree, they threw down their various loads of care in the place appointed. The resulting pile grew quickly into an enormous mountain. One man threw down his poverty, another his ill health, and another his unsavory reputation. There was a multitude of old people who with great delight threw down their wrinkles and their aches and pains. Many put down disabling worries, haunting fears, and distracting guilt complexes. A most interesting part of the procedure, Mr. Addison observed, was that many of the problems disposed of by this vast throng were more imaginary than real. Some threw down occupations they despised, and some used the opportunity to get rid of an incompatible spouse, a dominating parent, or a disobedient child.

While this confusion of miseries and chaos of calamities was taking place, Jupiter issued a second proclamation in which it was ordered that each one should pick up a new affliction in exchange for his old one and return to his own habitation. A poor galley slave who had thrown down his chains now replaced them with a case of gout. Some exchanged sickness for poverty and some traded hunger for a lack of appetite. Some traded care for pain, and some traded pain for care. Mr. Addison describes the pitiful condition thus created when the items that made up the mountain of miseries had been securely fastened upon the backs of the wrong people. The whole area was now filled with even more pitiful groans and lamentations as the sufferers wandered along under the severe pains of their new and more critical agonies. Finally Jupiter took compassion upon them and ordered them a second time to lay down their loads, this time with the design of everyone taking back his own miseries so that each could be tolerably happy again.

There are several important applications of this constructive idea. God has made available for us his own finest secrets of success. He has piled up for our use a great mountain of virtues, religious doctrines, ideas, abilities, attitudes, and personality traits, from which we may endlessly draw according to our desire. He has given us four great volumes of scripture, which we may study, memorize, and practice to our heart's content. He has ordained one day each week as the Sabbath day. We may go to the house of the Lord on that holy day he has set apart and work diligently and endlessly in the interests of our own eternal exaltation. He has ordained that through the law of repentance we may discard all those sins and bad attitudes that cause our problems without the necessity of picking up the sins and problems of anybody else.

We may not be able to share the bank account of John D. Rockefeller; but if we live every one of the principles of the gospel, we will have more material wealth than we need anyway, and in addition we can cut ourselves as large a share as we desire of the treasures of heaven.

Wise
Unto Salvation

Among the important people figuring in the account of the birth of Jesus were the wise men who came from the East to honor him. There were probably many other men living in the East and in the West at that time who could also properly be classified as wise men, but these particular wise men seemed to have had greater motivation to be wise in the ways of the Lord. Because of their past interests and accomplishments, they had studied the divine program and knew of the far-reaching effect of the Savior's birth.

The apostle Paul was speaking to a later wise man when he wrote to Timothy and said, ". . . from a child thou hast known the holy scriptures, which are able to make thee wise unto salvation through faith which is in Christ Jesus." (2 Timothy 3:15.) There are many things that can help us in this important objective, to be wise unto salvation. One is the study of the scriptures mentioned by Paul to his young disciple. The Lord himself has said, "Study to shew thyself approved unto God, a workman that needeth not be ashamed, rightly dividing the word of truth." (2 Timothy 2:15.) Another way in which we arrive at this same end is through industry. We learn to do by doing.

If you had your choice of what kind of wisdom would be most profitable to you, what would it be? Thomas Carlyle said, "A man's religion is the most important thing about him. That is what he thinks about, and believes in, and works at, and fights for, and lives by." A man's religion also determines what his eternal life will be like. Therefore, how important it is that we become wise in the ways of the Lord!

Becoming wise takes thought and effort. Even dreamers have little value unless their dreams are undergirded with both a plan and a program. The poet has said:

I may as well kneel down and worship gods of stone.
As offer to the living God a prayer of words alone.

Prayer can also be of great benefit. But prayer should never be mistaken as a substitute for thinking. If there are two men of equal intellectual power and both pray but only one is fully devoted to industry, there will be a great disparity between the accomplishments of the two, everything else being equal. It must always remain a fundamental truth that "the hands that help are holier than the lips that merely pray." Leonardo da Vinci gave us a thought-provoking prayer when he said, "Thou, Oh God, doth sell us all good things at the price of labor."

Studying, thinking, and reading should all be regular emotional experiences. If an idea in the mind does not arouse an emotion in the heart, it is unlikely that it will get out into the activity muscles. Before success can take place, the imagination must be stirred and set on fire. There must be a preliving of one's success, and every fantasy must be grounded in some measure of reality before it can take off for greater accomplishment.

The apostle Paul said that the scriptures are able to make us wise unto salvation, but some good mental emotions and some effective appraisals of values can also make us wise unto salvation. We must look forward as well as backward. One of the things that keeps each of us going is our ability to dream and aspire effectively. Sometimes we can wish things so intently that they happen. But we need to do a lot of dome work as well as home work. We need to get our hearts into the act. We also need to get ourselves oriented to righteousness if we are going to be wise unto salvation.

Index

Abraham, 140-41
Addison, Joseph, 211-13
Alchemists, 207-8
Alfred the Great, 205
Alma, 122
"American Women—A Sad Success Story," 152-53
Angels, 141
Animals, 197-98
Apocrypha, 1
Appreciation, 53
Areopagus, 86
Aristotle, 204-5
Atheism, 34-35
Athens, Socrates in, 26; court in, 86
Attitude, 80, 144-45
Automobile, telestial, 161
Aviator, 77-78

Bacon, Francis, 105
Barrie, James M., 163
Barrymore, Ethel, 164
Baseball manager, 206
Baum, Frank, 46
Beatitudes, 69
Beecher, Henry Ward, 179
Beggars, 44
Ben-Sira's Book of Wisdom, 2
Bible, 4-8
Bitterness, 171-72
Blaming others, 172
Bodies, 147
Books, 103
Boy Scout pledge, 57-58
Brain, 196
Bronowski, 38
"Brotherly Love," 92-93
Builder, 158-59
Building, 155
Burdick, Eugene, 78

Butler, Nicholas Murray, 32

Candy store, 63
Carnegie, Andrew, 100
Carlyle, Thomas, 158, 214
Change in people, 102-4
Character, development of, 56-57; negative, traits, 58; godly, 157
Children, 141
Children of God, 140
Children of light, 99, 101
Christ, as creator and teacher, 8-9; peace of, 70
Christmas Carol, 125
Cicero, 50
Clover, 133
Coleridge, Samuel, 186
Colton, 60
Commandments, 110
Comparisons, Jesus taught through, 74, 75-76
Conscience, 108
Coolidge, Calvin, 113
Corrigan, Douglas, 77-78
Courage, 50
Creation, 159-60, 167-69, 193, 198
Creditor, 109-10

David, father of Solomon, 20-21, 127
Death, 143
Debtor, 109-10
Degrees of glory, 161
Demosthenes, 112
Devil, 122
Diamond Jubilee, 94
Dickens, Charles, 125
Dirt, 191-92

216

Discipline of self, 28-29
Disraeli, Benjamin, 113
Domination, 39-40
Drinking, 124, 187
Drummond, Henry, 55

Economic welfare, 208
Edison, Thomas A., 49
Eisenhower, Dwight D., 60
Emerson, Ralph Waldo, writings
  of, 5; on character, 58; on
  writing, 61-62; on courtesy,
  83; on wisdom, 101; on
  intelligence, 210
Emotion, 60-61
England, 94
Enoch, 208-9
Equality, 146, 148
Eternal life, 18
Evil, 123-25
Example, as a teacher, 11;
  power of, 104
Experience, as a teacher, 10
Eyesight, 199

Fairbanks, Douglas, Jr., 164
Faith, of Job, 16-17; as a pillar,
  157
Family, 148
Farmer, 143
Fear, 61
Fear of the Lord, 3, 20
Fool, 86-87
Foolishness, characteristics of,
  23, 25
Football player, 77
Forger, 187
Forster, E. M., 83
Franklin, Benjamin, 92-93
Free agency, 160
Freedom, limitations of, 137; as
  a pillar, 157
Friends, 104

Garfield, James A., 61

Genius, 111-16
George, Lloyd, 60
Gettysburg Address, 126-27
Gibeon, 21
Giza, Sphinx of, 37-38
Gluttony, 62-64
God, nation built on belief in, 4;
  Solomon asked, for wisdom,
  21-23; opposition to, in
  schools, 33-35; man in image
  of, 41; character of, 56-57; and
  creation, 167-69; word of, 202
Goethe, 83, 174
Gold, 203-4
Goodell, Dr., 158
Governments, 103, 127
Gratitude, 50-51, 53
Greece, 204-5
Greek myth of Sphinx, 36
Grost, Mike, 111
Gurney, J. J., 60
Gustav, king of Sweden, 51

Hale, Edward Everett, 144-45
Hamilton, Alexander, 112
Hands, 49-50
Hebrews, 1
Henley, William Ernest, 117-18
Hesiod, 205
Hobab, 6-7
Hogan, Ben, 113
Homer, 202, 204
Houses we build, 155-58
Hubbard, Elbert, 113, 142, 166
Hugo, Victor, 176
Human nature, knowledge of, 2
Human suffering, purpose of,
  16
Husband, who wished to
  dominate, 40; who was
  irresponsible, 59; who hid
  from own problems, 120-21

Ideas, 176
Ignorance results in wickedness,
  28-29

Immortality of the soul, 27
Industry, as a teacher, 10-11; as a pillar, 157
Ingratitude, 53
Intelligence, 48-49; 107-8
"Invictus," 118
Irrigation reservoir, 132-33
Isaiah, 8
Israel at Mount Sinai, 96-97

James, William, 48
Jerusalem, Jesus' last days in, 129-30
Jesus, preexistence of, 12; early life of, 13; teachings of, 14-15; taught through parables, 74, 75-76; before crucifixion, 129-30; birth of, 141
Joan of Arc, 85, 119-20
Job, character of, 15-16; faith of, 16-17, 18-19; mediated, 19; concerning wisdom, 19-20
Judgment according to works, 130

Kelty, M. A., 83
King Gustav of Sweden, 51
Kipling, Rudyard, 94-96
Knowledge, of self, 29-30; love of, 103; sin against, 108-9

Laodicea, 134-35
Law of consecration, 208
Lederer, William, 78
Letter to "trouble" column, 90
Limitations of freedom, 137
Lincoln, Abraham, biblical values of, 4; on attitude, 68; genius of, 115; Gettysburg Address, 126-27; on his mother, 151; on looks, 160; on solving problems, 189
Link, Dr. Henry C., 9
Liquor, 124
Literature and the Bible, 5

Loneliness, 190
Lord, fear of, 3; on Mount Sinai, 96-97
Love, 49, 156
Lucifer, 78, 136

Man with the Hoe, 81
Mann, Horace, 103
Maple syrup harvest compared to moods, 62
Markham, Edwin, 81, 159
Marriage, 142, 169
Marshall, Peter, 44
Maturity, 164-66
McCreary, 194-95
McKay, David O., 66, 102, 162
Mead, Margaret, 152
Meditation, 19
Milton, John, 138, 201
Mind, 48, 68
Moods, 60-63
Morgan, J. P., 60
Moses, crossing the desert, 6-7; introduction of Jesus to, 141
Mothers, 148-50
Mount Sinai, 96-97
"Mountain of Miseries," 211-13
Myth of the Sphinx, 36

Napoleon, 148
Needs, 190
New Jerusalem, 203-4
Newspaper corporation, 182-83
Nightingale, Earl, 111

Occupations, 103, 142
"Ode on Intimations of Immortality," 107
Oedipus, 36-37
Olympic Games, 51
Orchard, 133

Parable by Benjamin Franklin, 92-93

Telestial automobile, 161
Temple built by Solomon,
127-30
Temptation, 179, 188
Tennyson, 5
Thebes, Sphinx of, 36-37
Thinking, 49, 215
Thorpe, Jim, 51-53
Thoughtlessness, 84
"Three Little Pigs," 156
Time machine, 67
Topsoil, 192-93
Tree of knowledge, 193
"Trouble" column, letter to, 90
Truth, 156

Ugly American, 78
Understanding, Solomon asked
for, 22-23
University, purpose of, 31-32;
teaching of atheism in, 33-34
Utopia, 209-10

Vegetation, 197
Vices, 131
Victoria, queen of England,
94-95
Vinci, Leonardo da, 113, 215
Violence, 38-39

Virtues, 131, 204

Wars, 70
Weaknesses, 120
Wealth, wisdom can produce,
19-20
Wealthy man, 158-59
Webster, Daniel, 103
Wells, H. G., 67
Wickedness as result of
ignorance or sloth, 28-29
Wilde, Oscar, 41, 149
Will, 64
Wilson, Woodrow, 48-49
Wisdom, human, 2; in the
teachings of Christ, 14-15; the
"price" of, 19-20; Solomon
asked for, 21-22; Solomon
lost, 24-26; as greatest thing,
55; where, found, 101
Wisdom literature, 1-3
Wise man, 155
Wordsworth, William, 107
Wright, Orville, 66, 99
"Wrong-way Corrigan," 77-78

Young, Brigham, 124
Young man and trust fund,
79-80